A Draught of the Sea Coasts of Holland and Parts Adjoin:
:ing, as they are Supposed to have been in Antient Times.
GERMANY
OF
Emden
Ameland I.
Grind
Dockum
Dam
Delfzyl
Groningen
GRONINGEN
Winschoten
Bourtanger F.
Franeker
Leuwarden
Bolswaert
Sneek
Worcum
Slooten
FRIS: LAND
OVER ISSEL
Meppel
Coevorden
Kurnder
Emeloort
Vollenhoven
Swart Sluys
Zwol
Hardenberg
Hatten
Rysen
Almeloo
Ootmersom
Deventer
Oldenzyl
Elburg
Harderwick
Loo
Amersfort
Zutphen
Borkelo
Lochem
Groel
Lichtenvoordt
Doesburg
Rhenen
Arnhem
Bredevoordt
Nimeguen
Tiel
Bommel
Ravestein
Schenk
Cleves
Rhine R.
Wesel
Coesfelt
Munster
Osnabrug
Lemgow
Hamme
Paderborn
Dorsten
Lippe R.
Lippe
Grave
Gelder
Rheinberg
Dortmund
Oirschot
Helmont
Eyndhoven
Kessel
Venlo
Duysburg
Horn
Weert
Ruremond
Erkelens
Dusseldorp
Nuys
B. OF LIEGE
Maeseyck
Mastricht
Borchloen
Tongres
Liege
Wyck
Dalem
LIMBURG
Valkenburg
Rolduck
Aix la Chapelle
Limburg
Juliers
Roer R.
Franchimont
Huy
Mouse R.
Spau
Stablo
Durbuy
Salmeville
St. Vit
La Roche en Famine & en Ardenne
Rochfort
Homfalize
St. Hubert
Clerveaux
Bastogne
Vianden
LUXEMBURG
Bovillon
Echternach
Triers
Arlon
Chiny
Luxemburg
Montmedy
Virton
Thionville
Mosell
Damvillers
Salæ Ostium item Flevum sive Orientale Rheni Ostium
Flevum Castellum
Amisia
GERMANIÆ PARS
BRUC
TERI
MAJORES
FRISII
MINORES
Monarmanis Portus
Lugdunum
Trajectus
Arenacum
MARSACI
Medium & verum sive Antiquissimum Rheni Ostium
Mosæ Ostium: item Helium sive Occidentale Rheni Ostium
Scaldis Ostium verum sive Antiquissimum
BAT
Batavodurum
Mosa fl.
Rhenus fl.
Sala sive Isala fl.
Fossa Drusi
Amisius fl.
GALLIÆ
BELGICÆ PARS
MENAPII
E
6
F
7
G
8
H
9
53
52
51
50
b
c
d
e
f
g
h

Logbook of the Low Countries

A chronicle of their historic moments
set against events in world history
featuring highlights from art and science
and illustrated with famous quotations

Compiled by
Wout van der Toorn

Seaside Publishing
The Hague

Book design: 2-D'sign, Amersfoort
Cover design: Marlies van Muiswinkel, Igor Design, The Hague
Production: tienstuks.nl, Amstelveen

Seaside Publishing
seaside.publishing@vandertoorn.nl
www.seasidepublishing.com

ISBN 978 90 8860 052 4
NUR 680

Logbook of the Low Countries

For my Muse, Cora

'The longer you can look back, the further you can see forward'
Sir Winston Churchill

Contents

Preface

History is once again enjoying the warm interest of a wide audience. This can be seen by the number of history books (both for adults and children) which appear every year, as well as by the steady stream of films, radio and television programmes.

A brief surf on the internet quickly results in numerous sites devoted to historical subjects. Newspapers from the 17th century, film images of Queen Victoria or a news summary from 1970 – with just a few clicks we can magically make them appear on our computer screens or mobile phones.

This is fantastic and handy of course. However, if people lack a historical overview they can soon get lost in this sea of information. Where should they begin their search and which search terms should they use? What happened in other countries at the same time?

Logbook of the Low Countries by Wout van der Toorn provides an answer to these questions. The major events from the history of Belgium, Luxembourg and The Netherlands are arranged chronologically in the first column, next to the high and low points from the history of the wider world in the second column.

In just one glance you can see that William, Prince of Orange-Nassau, later King William I of The Netherlands, landed on the beach of Scheveningen in 1813, while in that same year the Battle of the Nations took place near Leipzig and Jane Austen published her novel *Pride and Prejudice*. In short, *Logbook of the Low Countries* is a very handy 'timetable' (in itself an almost historic phenomenon) which logically leads you through world history.

Brussels and The Hague have both played an important role in the rich history of the Low Countries. At the time of the United Kingdom of The Netherlands, the centre of government alternated between Brussels and The Hague. And the European Congress in the Knights' Hall of The Hague in1948 started the process of European unification, which quickly became inseparable from the name of the city of Brussels.

It is therefore with great pleasure that we have agreed to write a preface to this book. We do sincerely hope that *Logbook of the Low Countries* will find a broad audience and will contribute to the wider dissemination of historical knowledge.

Jozias van Aartsen Mayor of The Hague	Brigitte Grouwels Minister of Brussels-Capital Region

Introduction

When talking to people from the wider world about the history of my country, I have often noticed that many are unaware of the significant developments which have taken place in the Low Countries over the centuries. This book has been written with the intention to fill this gap.

For centuries, the great rivers Rhine, Meuse and Scheldt formed the northern limes (border) of the Roman Empire and brought culture from various corners of Europe to the Belgae in this outpost. In the Dark Ages Frisians, Batavians and Gauls lived here during the reign of Charlemagne, occasionally invaded by the Vikings.

In the sixteenth century Flanders enjoyed its Golden Age, while Holland followed suit one century later. A struggle by the tiny Low Countries for religious freedom led to the Eighty-Years' War against the mighty Spanish Empire. The northern Netherlands victory resulted in the first modern democratic republic, which set the example for many other democracies around the world. The Republic of the Seven United Provinces developed into a leading world power, with colonies in the East and the West.

'These days it's often forgotten that the Dutch once presided over the world's pre-eminent maritime trading empire, the immediate predecessor to Britain's', wrote Amy Chua in her book: *Day of Empire*. Amy Chua gave as the main reason for this rise: 'By far the most crucial factor underlying the Dutch surge to global primacy was an extraordinary economic explosion. It was here that the Dutch Republic's exceptional policies of religious tolerance proved indispensable.' I should hasten to add that this development was only made possible by the influx of capable people and their capital from Flanders and other surrounding countries.

In modern times, Belgium, Luxembourg and The Netherlands have played a major role, first in the creation of the Benelux and later of the European Union and its many projects, including the euro.

During the twenty centuries it has taken to develop the Low Countries, there has always been an undeniable bond between their northern and southern parts. Professor Hugo De Schepper points out that: 'Even after the separation in 1648, the history of North and South are intertwined not only in name, but also by the continuation of their intense economic and cultural relationship.'

To arrive at a concise chronicle of the Low Countries I have followed the concept of George Courtauld's *Pocket Book of Patriotism.* In two parallel columns a chronological summary of important events in the Low Countries is set against events in the wider world in order to show their relationship. As in Courtauld's book, the timelines are interspersed with quotations from the relevant period. Quotations in languages other than English are given with a translation.

Of the 2,500 or so references in the main text, about one third relate to the history of the Low Countries. Not only kings and conflicts, but also achievements in art, science and technology are highlighted.
In general, each reference gives the year or the period during which the event took place, a brief description of the event and separated by a semicolon, an indication of its consequences.

I hope that the inclusion of a relatively large number of references to events outside Europe, particularly to the Middle East, Central Asia, India, China and Japan gives appropriate emphasis to the growing importance of these regions.

An unusual word is 'Stadholder', used between 1500 and 1800. This term originally referred to the representative of the King of France or Spain, who entrusted part of their possessions into the hands of a feudal lord (e.g. the Duke of Flanders or the Count of Holland). In order to keep an eye on his feudal lords, the king appointed his own representative. In German, such a person is called 'Statthalter' (meaning: 'instead holding'). In Dutch this becomes 'Stadhouder' and in English 'Stadtholder'.
Later on this title was used for any person who represents the ultimate power in a province.

For lesser-known towns, rivers and regions, the country where they are now located, is mentioned, abbreviated and in parenthesis. However, for greater accuracy, in the Low Countries, the present province is mentioned instead. A list of the provinces of the Low Countries can be found in the appendices.

This book contains separate subject indexes, which refer to a particular year or period (rather than a page number) in the main text. I have also included the texts of the national anthems of the Low Countries and a list of their (former) colonial possessions. I trust this book will help the reader to find the historic highlights easily and quickly. It does not claim to explain the course of events, but nevertheless gives the context within which the events took place.

I should like to thank Joan McNamara, Martien Braber, Peter Loader and Jacques Zonneveld for their useful remarks and practical assistance with the subtleties of the Queen's English.

Wout van der Toorn OBE,
The Hague, March 2012

簡介

在與外國人談起我祖國的歷史的時候，我發現很多人不了解低地國家這幾個世紀所取得的重大發展。所以我寫這本書的目的，就是爲了填補衆人在荷蘭歷史上的知識空缺。

萊茵河、斯海爾德河、默茲河形成了日耳曼帝國北方的邊界，並且把文化從歐洲各地引入了居住在此地的　爾格族人的生活之中，到了歐洲中世紀的黑暗時代，在查理曼大帝國統治下的弗里斯人，巴達？人和高盧人還時不時跟日耳曼人有着往來。

到了十六世紀，弗爾德迎來了它的黃金時代，一個世紀之後荷蘭郡也開始跟了上來。這些弱小的低地國家爲了取得宗教上的獨立，和強大的西班牙打了一場長達八十年的戰爭，這些北部低地國家的勝利宣告了第一個現代民主共和國的誕生，並爲全世界很多其他的民主國家樹立了榜樣。

烏德勒支同盟等七省組合共和國，隨後發展成爲世界上領先的大國，其殖民地遍佈東方和西方。

美耶魯大家終身教授蔡美儀在她的書《帝國時代：超級強國如何成爲主宰及失敗的原因》中寫道："現在人們已經忘了這一個事實，即荷蘭曾經是統治着世界海上貿易的帝國，然後才是英國，" 她還指出了其崛起的原因："到目前爲止普遍認爲荷蘭崛起爲世界重要大國的原因之一是其非凡的經濟發展，這跟荷蘭共和國實行宗教寬容的好政策是分不開的。"

在這裏我要補充一點，就是各地人才的到來和弗爾德及其周邊國家的資本的湧入使得荷蘭我發展成爲可能。

到了現代，比利時、盧森堡和荷蘭三國在比荷盧經濟聯盟中扮演重要角色，隨後又在歐盟及其下屬機構，包括歐元的推行上都起着重要的作用。

在低地國家的 2000 多年的發展過程中，北部和南部國家之間的關系舉足輕重。正如 Hugo De Schepper 教授所說的："雖然北部和南部於 1648 年分裂，但兩地的歷史還是緊密地連系在一起。這不僅是因爲兩地的名稱有着相同之處，更是因爲兩地之間從未中斷的密切的貿易往來和文化連系。

寫作時我遵循了喬治、科陶德所著《帝國主義小冊子》一書中的框架，當中有兩個平行的方框，其中一個方框是低地國家的歷史上發生的重大事件，另一個方框內的是世界歷史上發生的重大事件。這些事件均是按時先後次序排列，並且兩個方框內相同時段發生的事件放在一起，以體驗出它們之間的關系。此外，這些大事年表中還附上了相同時期的重要引文，除了英文以外的引文外都有相關的翻譯。

正文中 2500 多條的引文中，差不多有一半是和低地國家的歷史有關的。這些引文不僅僅是跟國王和戰爭有關，還涉及了學術、科學和技術方面取得的成就，基本的排版就是先指出年份，接着是有在這一年發生的重大事件的概述，然後是這些事件所帶來的影響。

除了歐洲的引文外，我還搜集了大量來自中東、中亞、印度、中國和日本的引文，以顯示這些地區在當今世界發展中的重要性。

在英語中一個不尋常的用詞—"Stadtholder"，在 1500 至 1800 年間被頻繁使用。這個詞最初指的是法國、德國或者西班牙國王所派遣的代表。這些國王把自己一部份權力委託給各封建地主(如弗爾德公爵，荷蘭郡伯爵等)。除了委任這些封建地主，國王委派了一位代表，在德語裏面這樣的代表被稱爲"Statthalter"(意思爲"代替持有")，在荷蘭語裏這樣的人是被稱爲"Stadthouder"，在英語裏就是"Stadtholder"。到後來這個字就被用來代表荷蘭的省內持有最高權力的人，即省長。

無論什麼時候，不管在世界任何地方，將來再有一個新發明或新發現，即使這個發明或者新發現是原有或原創的，我會把在時間上稍晚出現的，但意思相同的稱爲"改寫"。

這本書也談到一些較不知名的市鎮，河流和地區，並說明其現今的所在地。若這些地點是在今日的荷蘭，將列明其所隸屬的省份。本書提供了荷蘭省份的清單。

這本書設置了獨立的單獨主題索引，以相應的年份（而不是頁碼）回應主要的文本。我也在本書中紀錄了低地國家國歌的歌詞和列出他們的許多前殖民地的清單。

我相信這本書將有助讀者很容易和快速地找到歷史的亮點。它的主要功能不是解釋事件發生的過程，而是展示事件發生的事實和範圍。

我在此特別感謝 Joan MacNamara 女士 和 Peter Loader 先生對本書的有用評論和協助本書小標題的皇室英語翻譯工作。

Wout van der Toorn OBE, 寫於海牙, 2011 年 1 月。

Introduction

Au cours de conversations avec des étrangers sur l'histoire de mon pays, j'ai pu observer chez beaucoup la méconnaissance des évolutions majeures ayant marqué les « Bas Pays » au cours des siècles passés. Ce livre a été écrit dans l'intention de combler ce déficit de connaissance de l'histoire des Pays-Bas.

Les grands fleuves, le Rhin, la Meuse et l'Escaut, qui ont formé pendant des siècles le *limes* (la frontière) nord de l'empire romain, ont apporté la culture de divers coins de l'Europe aux *Belgae* installés dans cet avant-poste. Au Haut Moyen-Âge, sous le règne de Charlemagne, y vécurent Frisons, Bataves et Gaulois, recevant à l'occasion la visite des Normands.

C'est au seizième siècle que la Flandre a vécu son âge d'or, suivie un siècle plus tard par la Hollande. La lutte pour la liberté religieuse a conduit à la guerre de Quatre-vingts ans contre la domination espagnole. La victoire des Bas Pays du nord a mené à la création de la première république démocratique moderne, qui a servi d'exemple pour de nombreuses autres démocraties dans le monde entier.

Le développement de la république des sept Provinces Unies en fit alors la première puissance du monde, avec ses colonies en Orient et en Occident.
« De nos jours, on oublie souvent que les Hollandais ont été dans le passé à la tête du principal empire maritime et commercial du monde, prédécesseurs immédiats des Britanniques » écrit Amy Chua dans son livre *Day of Empire*. Amy a donné à cet essor une raison: « Le facteur déterminant ayant sous-tendu la suprématie globale des Hollandais fut, de loin, une explosion extraordinaire de leur économie. C'est là que l'exceptionnelle politique de tolérance religieuse de la république hollandaise s'est révélée indispensable ».
Je dois m'empresser d'ajouter que ce développement n'a été rendu possible que par l'afflux de personnes capables et de leurs capitaux, depuis la Flandre et les autres pays environnants.

De nos jours, la Belgique, le Luxembourg et les Pays-Bas ont joué un rôle important, d'abord dans la création du Benelux puis plus tard dans celle de l'Union européenne et de ses nombreuses institutions, y compris l'Euro.

Le lien entre les parties septentrionales et méridionales des Bas Pays au cours des vingt siècles de leur développement est indéniable.
Selon le professeur Hugo de Schepper, « Même après la séparation en 1648, l'histoire du nord et celle du sud sont entremêlées non seulement par leur nom, mais encore par la poursuite de leurs relations économiques et culturelles intenses».

Aussi ai-je décidé de suivre le schéma du livre *Pocket Book of Patriotism* de George Courtauld. Sur deux colonnes parallèles, sont placés en vis-à-vis les événements importants de l'histoire des Pays-Bas et ceux du vaste monde afin d'en faire ressortir les liens réciproques. Comme dans le livre de Courtauld, la chronologie est émaillée de maximes de la période considérée. Les citations en une langue autre que l'anglais sont accompagnées d'une traduction.

Environ le tiers des quelques 2 500 références du texte principal se rapportent à l'histoire des Bas Pays. L'accent est mis non seulement sur les rois et les conflits, mais aussi sur les réalisations dans le domaine des arts, de la science et de la technologie. En règle générale, l'année mentionnée est suivie d'une courte description de l'événement et d'une indication de ses conséquences.

J'espère, par l'inclusion d'un nombre relativement important de références à des événements extérieurs à l'Europe, touchant en particulier le Moyen-Orient, l'Asie Centrale, l'Inde, la Chine et le Japon, avoir souligné de manière appropriée l'importance croissante de ces régions.

Un mot inhabituel est celui de « Stadtholder », employé souvent entre les années 1500 et 1800. Ce terme se rapporte à l'origine à la personne représentant le roi de France, ou d'Espagne, dont une partie des possessions est tenue par des seigneurs féodaux, par exemple le duc de Flandre ou le comte de Hollande. Afin de garder un œil sur ces seigneurs, le souverain nomme un représentant, appelé en allemand « Statthalter », ce qui signifie littéralement « Lieu-tenant ». En néerlandais, ce mot est devenu « Stadhouder » et en anglais « Stadtholder ». Ultérieurement, ce titre désigne toute personne représentant la puissance souveraine dans une province.

Pour les villes, cours d'eau et régions peu connus, mention est faite des pays dans lesquels ils se trouvent actuellement. Cependant, dans les Pays-Bas, c'est la province qui est mentionnée. La liste des provinces des Pays-Bas est fournie.

Ce livre contient des index séparés par thèmes, qui renvoient dans le corps de l'ouvrage à une ou plusieurs dates particulières (de préférence à un numéro de page). J'ai également inclus les paroles des hymnes nationaux des Pays-Bas et une liste de leurs (anciennes) possessions coloniales.

Ce livre, je l'espère, aidera le lecteur à trouver facilement et rapidement les points marquants de l'histoire. Sans prétendre expliquer le cours des événements, il donne néanmoins le contexte dans lequel ces événements ont eu lieu.

Je voudrais remercier Joan McNamara, Martien Braber, Peter Loader et Jacques Zonneveld pour leurs remarques utiles et leur soutien pratique au travers des subtilités académiques de la langue de Shakespeare.

Wout van der Toorn,
La Haye, Novembre 2011

Einleitung

Während Gesprächen mit Ausländern über die Geschichte meines Landes, bemerke ich oft, dass viele Leute über die bedeutenden Entwicklungen, die in den Niederlanden während der vergangenen Jahrhunderte stattfanden, nicht informiert sind.
Dieses Buch wurde mit der Absicht geschrieben, diese Wissenslücken über die Niederlande zu füllen.

Die großen Flüsse Rhein, Maas und Schelde bildeten den Limes (Grenze) des römischen Reiches für Jahrhunderte.
Sie transportierten aber auch die Kultur von den verschiedensten Ecken Europas nach Belgae - diesem Vorposten der Römer. Im Mittelalter lebten Friesen, Batavar und Gallier hier unter der Herrschaft von Karl dem Großen, gelegentlich bekamen sie Besuch von den Normannen.

Im fünfzehnten Jahrhundert erlebte Flandern das Goldene Zeitalter, während Holland ein Jahrhundert später folgte. Der Kampf für die Religionsfreiheit löste den Achtzig-Jährigen Krieg gegen die spanische Unterdrückung aus. Der Sieg für die Nördlichen Niederlande führte zur Entstehung der ersten modernen demokratischen Republik, der Republik der Vereinigten Niederlande, die das Beispiel für viele andere Demokratien in der Welt darstellen sollte.

Die Republik der sieben Vereinigten Provinzen entwickelte sich zur führenden Weltmacht, mit Kolonien im Osten und im Westen der Welt. „Heutzutage wird häufig vergessen, dass Holland einmal das dominierende Handels- und Weltreich war, noch vor Großbritannien das wurde“, schrieb Amy Chua in ihrem Buch: „*Day of Empire*“. Amy nannte als Grund für diesen Aufstieg der Niederlande: „Der wichtigste Faktor für den holländischen Sprung zur Weltmacht war die außergewöhnliche ökonomische Entwicklung. Für diese außergewöhnliche ökonomische Entwicklung war die holländischen Politik der Republik der Niederlande in Form der Toleranz gegenüber Religionen unentbehrlich.“

Ich füge dem hinzu, dass diese prosperierende wirtschaftliche Entwicklung nur durch das Kommen der tüchtigen Händler und Menschen sowie ihres Kapitals vor allem aus Flandern und von anderen europäischen Ländern möglich wurde.

Auch in der Moderne Zeit spielten und spielen Belgien, Luxemburg und die Niederlande eine Hauptrolle in Europa. Zuerst mit der

Gründung der Benelux-Union und später als Gründungsmitglieder der Europäischen Union und seiner vielen Organisationen, einschließlich der Gemeinschaftswährung, dem Euro.

Im zwanzigsten Jahrhundert ist die enge Verbindung zwischen dem Nördlichen (Niederlande) und dem südlichen Teil (Flandern), die einst zusammen gehörten, wieder eine Tatsache. „Nach der Trennung der Nördlichen und der Südlichen Niederlande, durch den Frieden von Münster 1648, blieb die Geschichte des Nordens und Südens nicht nur im Namen und durch die Sprache, aber auch durch die Fortsetzung der intensiven ökonomischen und kulturellen Beziehungen eng miteinander verknüpft“, meint Prof. Hugo De Schepper.

In meinem Buch folge ich dem Ansatz von George Courtauld's Buches: *Pocket Book of Patriotism*“. In zwei parallelen Kolumnen wird eine chronologische Zusammenfassung der wichtigen Ereignisse in den Niederlanden gegeben, denen die Ereignisse in anderen Teilen der Welt gegenüber gestellt werden. Ziel ist es, die Beziehungen zwischen diesen Entwicklungen zu zeigen. Wie im Buch Courtauld's, werden die Zeitlinien garniert mit Aussagen von Prominenten jener Zeit. Sind sie nicht in Englisch, dann wurden sie übersetzt.

Von den etwa 2.500 Ereignissen, die im Haupttext dargestellt werden, beziehen sich ungefähr ein Drittel auf die Geschichte der Niederlande. Nicht nur Könige, Kriege und Konflikte, sondern auch Ereignisse in Bezug auf die Kunst, die Wissenschaften und die Technologie werden hervorgehoben. Im Allgemeinen wird erst das Jahr des Ereignisses mit einer kurzen Beschreibung des Ereignisses dargestellt und dann werden die Konsequenzen, die es brachte, beleuchtet.

Ich hoffe, dass die Einbeziehung einer verhältnismäßig großen Anzahl von Hinweisen auf Ereignisse außerhalb Europas, insbesondere im Nahen Osten, in Zentralasien, in Indien, China und Japan der wachsenden Bedeutung dieser Regionen gerecht wird.

Ein für Deutschsprachige Leser wohl eher unverständliches Wort ist: „Stadtholder.“ Es wird häufig benutzt in den Jahren 1500 bis 1800. Diese Bezeichnung meint ursprünglich eine Person, die den König von Frankreich, von Deutschland oder von Spanien repräsentierte. Dieser „Stadtholder“ sollte die Teile der königlichen Ländereien, die die Feudalherren, z.B. den Herzog von Flandern oder den Graf von Holland, vom jeweiligen König erhalten hatten, um sie zu verwalten bzw. zu regieren, kontrollieren. Auf Deutsch könnte man eine solche Perso: „Statthalter“ nennen. Auf Holländisch hieße sie: „Stadhouder“ und auf English: „Stadtholder“. Später wird dieser Titel für jede Person verwendet, die die entscheidende Macht in einer Provinz darstellte.

Für weniger bekannte Städte, Flüsse und Regionen wird das Land, in dem sie momentan lokalisiert werden, erwähnt. In den Niederlanden werden jedoch die Provinzen genannt. Eine Liste der Provinzen der Niederlande füge ich bei.

Dieses Buch enthält unterschiedliche Inhaltsverzeichnisse. Sie führen zu einem bestimmten Jahr (anstatt zur Seitenzahl) im Haupttext. Ich habe auch die Texte der nationalen Hymnen der Niederlande und die Liste ihrer (ehemaligen) Kolonien beigefügt.

Ich hoffe, dass dieses Buch dem Leser hilft, leicht und schnell die wichtigsten historischen Ereignisse zu finden. Ich beanspruche nicht, die Entstehungsgeschichte der Ereignisse zu erklären, aber möchte den Kontext, in dessen sie stattfanden, darstellen.

Ich danke Joan McNamara, Martien Braber, Peter Loader und Jacques Zonneveld für ihre nützlichen Anmerkungen und ihre praktische Unterstützung beim Durchdringen der Feinheiten der englischen Sprache der Königinnen – des ‚Queen's English‘.

Wout van der Toorn,
Den Haag, November 2011

Introducción

Hablando con extranjeros sobre la historia de mi país, me dí cuenta que muchas personas no conocen la evolución de los acontecimientos importantes que han tenido lugar durante siglos en los Países Bajos. Este libro ha sido escrito con la intención de ayudar a llenar el vacío de conocimiento que existe de cara a la historia del pasado de Holanda.

Los grandes ríos Rin, Mosa, Escalda formaron durante siglos las líneas fronterizas del Norte del Imperio Romano y fueron los que llevaron la cultura de varios rincones de Europa a los Belgas en este lugar. En las Edades Bárbaras los Frisos, Bátavos y Galos vivieron aquí bajo el Reinado de Carlos el Grande, ocasionalmente visitado por los Normandos.

En el siglo dieciséis Flandes experimentó su Edad de Oro, mientras que Holanda le siguió un siglo después. Una lucha por la libertad religiosa desencadenó la guerra de los ochenta años contra la dominación española. La victoria de los Países Bajos del Norte tuvo como consecuencia la creación de la primera república moderna que sirvió como ejemplo para muchas otras democracias alrededor del mundo.

La República de las Siete Provincias Unidas se convirtió en el líder del poder mundial con colonias en el Este y Oeste.

"Hoy en día se suele olvidar que los Holandeses presidieron el Imperio Marítimo de Negocios Mundial, el predecesor inmediato del Inglés" escribió Amy Chua en su libro: "*Day of Empire*". Amy alegó como motivo para este éxito: "Con mucha diferencia el factor más crucial del resurgimiento de los holandeses hacia la primacía global era una explosión económica extraordinaria. Aquí fue donde las excepcionales políticas holandesas respecto de la tolerancia religiosa mostraron ser indispensables".

Yo me apresuro a añadir que este desarrollo sólo fue posible por la influencia de personas competentes de Flandes y su capital y de otros países en los alrededores.

En los tiempos modernos, Bélgica, Luxemburgo y los Países Bajos han jugado un papel importante primero en la creación del Benelux y más adelante en la Unión Europea y sus muchas instituciones, incluido el Euro.

Innegable, durante los veinte siglos del desarrollo de los Países Bajos, es la unión entre su parte Norte y Sur. "Incluso después de la separación en 1648, la historia del Norte y Sur está entrelazada no sólo en el nombre pero también por la continuación de la intensa relación económica y cultural" según el Profesor Em. Hugo De Schepper.

Por este motivo he seguido el esquema del libro de George Courtauld: "*Pocket Book of Patriotism*". En dos columnas paralelas se plasma un resumen cronológico de los eventos más importantes en los Países Bajos en el marco de los acontecimientos en el resto del mundo con el fin de mostrar la relación entre ellos. Al igual que en el libro de Courtauld, las líneas del tiempo están entremezcladas con citados del periodo correspondiente. Los citados en idiomas distintos al inglés están traducidos

De los 2,500 referencias o más que se dan en el texto principal, aproximadamente un tercio habla de la historia de los Países Bajos. No sólo habla de Reyes y conflictos, pero también se destacan las proezas en arte, ciencia y tecnología. En general a continuación del año figura una pequeña descripción del acontecimiento y una leyenda de sus consecuencias.

Espero que la inclusión de un número relativamente grande de referencias a eventos fuera de Europa, especialmente en Oriente Medio, Asia Central, India, China, y Japón enfaticen de forma apropiada la creciente importancia de estas regiones.

Una palabra inusual es: "Stadholder", que se utilizaba mucho entre 1500 y 1800. Esta terminología originalmente hacia referencia a la persona que representaba el Rey de Francia, Alemania o España, que confiaba parte de sus posesiones al lord feudal (por ejemplo el Duque de Flandes o el Conde Holanda). Con el fin de mantener controlados a sus lords feudales, el Rey nombra un representante. En Alemania se llama: "Statthalter" (que significa "en tenencia"). En Holanda se convirtió en: "Stadhouder" y en Inglés "Stadholter". Más adelante este título se utilizaba para cualquier persona que representaba el máximo poder en una provincia.

Para ciudades, ríos y regiones menos conocidas, se menciona el país donde se encuentran en la actualidad. Sin embargo en el caso de los Países Bajos, en su lugar se menciona la provincia. Se facilita una lista de las provincias en los Países Bajos.

Este libro contiene índices de sujetos separados que hacen referencia a un año o periodo en concreto (en lugar de poner número de página) en el texto principal. También he incluido los textos de los himnos nacionales de los Países Bajos y una lista de sus (antiguas) posesiones coloniales.

Confío que este libro sea de ayuda para el lector en aras a encontrar rápidamente y con facilidad los hechos históricos destacados. No pretende explicar el curso de los eventos, pero sin embargo facilitar el contexto en el cual los eventos tuvieron lugar

Me gustaría agradecer a Joan McNamara, Martien Braber, Peter Loader y Jacques Zonneveld sus comentarios útiles y su asistencia con la sutileza del idioma Inglés Real.

Wout van der Toorn,
La Haya, Noviembre 2011

Logbook of the Low Countries

*'In the beginning God created the heavens and the earth.
And the earth was without form and void'*
GENESIS, THE BIBLE

Old World

c 150,000 BC Glacial ice from Scandinavia covers the northern part of Europe

c 100,000 BC Humans (Homo sapiens) spread out from Africa to Eurasia
c 40,000 BC Neanderthal men appear in northwest Europe

c 30,000 BC First men settle on the fertile loess soil in the present province of Limburg

c 20,000 BC Men populate America from Asia

9500-4400 BC Melting water fills the low-lying plain between the European mainland and England; North Sea is formed and the coastline of the Low Countries defined

c 5500 BC Indo-Germanic tribes from around the river Volga (Rus.) move to Central Asia, Europe and India

c 5300 BC Agriculture comes to the southern Low Countries

c 4000 BC Metals, first copper then bronze, replace stone for tools

c 3500 BC Low Countries above the rivers Rhine and Meuse come under cultivation
c 3000 BC Hunebeds, large stone graves, appear in the present province of Drenthe

c 3150 BC King Menes unifies Egypt, several dynasties rule Egypt for the next three millennia; invention of hieroglyphic writing
3000-1400 BC Minoan civilisation settles on the island of Crete (Gr.)
2700-2200 BC *Old Kingdom Period* famous for its many pyramids in Egypt

Low Countries

Wider World

c 2630 BC Pharaoh Cheops erects his pyramid in Sakkara (Egyp.)
c 2500 BC Indus culture develops around Mohenjo-Daro in the Indus Valley (Pak.)
2070-1600 BC Xia dynasty rules China, *The Middle Kingdom;* King Yu (the Great) is the first ruler
c 2000 BC King Knossos builds his palace on the island of Crete (Gr.); centre of Minoan civilisation

2000-1700 BC Grave mounds with wooden piles appear in the present province of North Brabant

2000-1300 BC *Stonehenge* Megalithic monument with stones of up to forty tonnes erected in England
c 1820 BC Egyptians construct a right angle, using a triangle with sides to the ratio of 3: 4: 5
c 1850 BC Farmers in Babylon (Iraq) pay interest for advanced sowing seed; first record of interest in history
c 1800 BC Abraham, founding patriarch of the Jewish people, moves from Mesopotamia, area between the rivers Euphrates and the Tigris (Iraq), to Israel
c 1700 BC King Hammurabi of Babylon (Iraq) codifies the oldest law on earth

'An eye for an eye, a tooth for a tooth'
CODE OF HAMMURABI

1700-1500 BC Phoenicians, maritime traders from Lebanon, develop the alphabet
1500-500 BC Ancient Veda religion lays the foundation for Hinduism and the Caste system in India
1550-1050 BC Shang dynasty rules China around the Yellow River valley
1550-1070 BC Egypt expands to its greatest extent as an international power

1358-1350 BC Boy-King Tutankhamun rules Egypt
c 1250 BC 'Trojan War' between Athens (Gr.) and Troy (Turk.) described by Homer, Greek poet, in his peerless epics *The Iliad* and *The Odyssey*
c 1225 BC Prophet Moses leads the Jewish people out of Egypt; receives the *Ten Commandments*

'Thou shalt not kill'
SIXTH COMMANDMENT, EXODUS, THE BIBLE

1200-1000 BC Dorians, Ionians and Aeolians coming from the north, settle in Greece and Crete (Gr.)
c 1100 BC Phoenicians found Cadiz (Sp.); most ancient city still existing in western Europe
1050-256 BC Zhou dynasty rules China; use of iron introduced
c 1000 BC Nomads in Eurasiatic Steppe use horses for riding; the aristocratic horseman emerges
960-925 BC King Solomon rules Israel; temple in Jerusalem built
c 850 BC Celts settle in northern Gaul (Fr.)
c 850 BC Medes migrate from Central Asia to Iran
814 BC Carthage (Tun.) founded by Phoenicians
c 800 BC Etruscan civilisation emerges in northern Italy
c 800 BC Chinese invent printing with movable-type
c 800 BC Celts arrive in Britain
776 BC First Olympic Games held in Olympia (Gr.)
753 BC Legendary brothers Romulus and Remus found Rome
c 750 BC Persians migrate from Central Asia to southern Iran

c 750 BC Celtic culture emerges north of the Alps

c 700 BC Frisians build terps (clay hills) to flee high water

c 700 BC Introduction of iron for weapons and tools

From 700 BC Aristocracy dominates society

700-300 BC Scythes, Iranian nomads, dominate the Steppe of Russia
c 675 BC Lao Tzu, Chinese philosopher and founder of Taoism, writes *Tao Te Ching*
c 650 BC First Medes, then Persians migrate from Iran to Mesopotamia
630-553 BC Life of Zoroaster, Iranian prophet and philosopher; founder of the Zoroastrian religion
612 BC Babylonians and Medes from Mesopotamia defeat Assyrians; Nineveh, capital of Assyria (Iraq) falls
605 BC Nebuchadnezzar II, King of Babylon, defeats Pharaoh Necho II, who claims Assyria
604-562 BC Nebuchadnezzar II constructs the *Hanging Gardens of Babylon*
c 600 BC Pharaoh Necho II attempts to dig a canal from the river Nile (Egyp.) to the Red Sea
c 600 BC Chinese use arches for building constructions
c 600 BC Phoenicians navigate to southern England and southern Africa
586 BC Nebuchadnezzar II destroys the Temple of Jerusalem and forces the Jews into exile; end of the State of Israel
c 580-496 BC Life of Pythagoras, Greek mathematician; discovers the theorem relating to the sides of a right-angled triangle

$(a^2 + b^2 = c^2)$
PYTHAGORAS

c 566-486 BC Life of Gautama Buddha (the enlightened one), spiritual teacher in northeast India; founder of Buddhism (religion and philosophy)
559 BC King Cyrus accedes to the Persian throne and in 549 BC to the Medes throne
551-479 BC Life of Confucius, Chinese philosopher

Chi-lu spoke: 'May I ask about death?'
And the Master said: 'You do not even understand life.
How can you understand death?'
CONFUCIUS

c 550 BC Chinese Kaots'ang Wo-Shu makes a sailing carriage, which carries thirty people
550-330 BC Persian Empire, ruling over Greater Iran; the first world power in history
539 BC Cyrus, King of Persia, conquers Babylon; Jews return to Jerusalem
525 BC Persians defeat Egyptians
525-456 BC Life of Aeschylus, Greek tragedian, whose works include the play *Oresteia*; beginning of European literature
521-485 BC Darius I, King of Persia, expands his realm into Asia Minor and Indus valley
509 BC Cleisthenes, Athenian statesman, reforms the constitution; first steps towards democracy in Athens
c 500 BC Sun Tzu, Chinese general, writes *The Art of War*

'The general determines where the battle is fought, not the enemy and surely not fate'
SUN TZU

c 500 BC Batavians sail down the Rhine; settle on land between Rhine and Meuse (Gel.)

c 500 BC Darius I completes a canal between Nile and Red Sea

Classical Period

496-406 BC Life of Sophocles, Greek tragedian, his works include the play *Electra*
490 BC Greeks defeat Persians at Marathon (Gr.); runner reports the victory in Athens, 26.2 miles away
485-423 BC Life of the Greek Herodotus, world's first historian
484-406 BC Life of Euripides, Greek tragedian, famous for his play *Medea*
480 BC 'Battle of Thermopylae (Gr.)' Xerxes, King of Persia, with 500,000 soldiers defeats Leonidas, King of Sparta, who has only 300 soldiers

'Go tell them in Sparta, O passer-by, That here, in obedience to their orders, we lie'
EPITAPH, AS LACONIC AND STERN AS LEONIDAS HIMSELF, ON THE SITE OF THEIR LAST STAND

480 BC 'Battle of Salamis (Gr.)' Greeks with three hundred triremes (warship with three rows of oarsmen) defeat the Persian fleet in the Saronic Gulf (Gr.); turning point in the Persian Battle for western Europe
470-399 BC Life of Socrates, Greek philosopher, found guilty of corrupting the minds of the young; condemned to drink poison
462-429 BC Pericles, charismatic Greek statesman, orator and general; became first citizen of Athens
450-387 BC Life of Aristophanes, Greek comic playwright, best known for his play *Lysistrata*
431-404 BC 'Peloponnesian Wars' rage between Athens and Sparta; end with defeat of Athens
427-347 BC Life of Plato, classical Greek philosopher, mathematician and writer; founder of the school *Academy*

c 400 BC Celts occupy northern Italy; end of Etruscan culture
400-200 BC *Ramayana* Ancient epic in Sanskrit (Indo-European language) emerges in India
390 BC Gauls under Chieftain Brennus defeat Romans near the river Allia (It.) and threaten to conquer Rome; holy geese of the Capitol raise alarm
384-332 BC Life of Aristotle, Greek philosopher, and tutor to Alexander the Great

'Be a leader for the Greeks, but a tyrant to the barbarians'
ARISTOTLE TO THE YOUNG ALEXANDER

c 350 BC Maya civilisation rises in Central America
338 BC King Philip II of Macedonia defeats Greeks near Chaeronea (Gr.) after consulting the *Oracle of Delphi*
334-331 BC Alexander III (the Great), King of Macedonia, conquers Egypt and Syria, then conquers Persia and northwest India.
305-285 BC Ptolemy I, Alexander's friend, reigns as Satrap over Egypt
c 300 BC Turk-Mongol peoples adopt the nomadic lifestyle and become horse-riders

c 300 BC Cananefaten settle in the northern coastal dunes, Belgae settle south of the rivers Rhine and Meuse

280 BC King Pyrrhus of Epirus (Gr.) defeats the Romans at Heracla (It.) but with heavy losses; resulting in the expression *Pyrrhic victory*, for victory obtained at too great a cost.
272-232 BC King Asoka (the Great) unites Indian subcontinent; erects rock edicts with inscriptions about behaviour and freedom across the country
264-146 BC 'Punic Wars' rage between Rome and Carthage

221-206 BC Qin dynasty rules China; construction of the *Great Wall*, standardisation of weights, measurements, currencies and writing systems
221-214 BC BC Emperor Qin Shi Huang; constructs mausoleum in Xi'an featuring eight thousand terracotta soldiers
218 BC Hannibal, Carthaginian military commander, crosses the Alps into Italy on war elephants
217 BC Hannibal defeats the Romans near Cannae (It.); stops short of conquering Rome
206 BC- 220 AD Han dynasty rules in China; golden age in Chinese history
c 200 BC Romans use arches in building constructions, as the Chinese did before
c 200 BC Chinese describe the circulation of blood with the heart as a pump with two separate bloodstreams
c 150 BC Cato the Elder, Roman senator, concludes each speech with

'... ceterum censeo Carthaginem esse delendam!'
'... moreover, I think that Carthage must be destroyed!', CATO THE ELDER

146 BC Carthage destroyed by the Romans
101 BC Teutons, a Germanic tribe from Denmark, invade Italy; Gaius Marius, Roman general, defeats the Teutons near Aix-en-Provence (Fr.)
c 100 BC Eudoxus of Cyzicus, Egyptian merchant, sails to India via Bab el Mandeb (Red Sea) and Strait of Hormuz (Persian Gulf); learns to use the trade winds
c 100 BC Nomads in the Sahara use camels
c 100 BC Chinese use decimal fractions and the number zero
c 100 BC Sima Qian, prefect of the Scribes, records the history of China from its beginning
88 BC Mithridates I, King of Pontus (Turk.), invades Asia Minor and occupies Athens

88 BC Lucius Sulla, Roman general and Consul, negotiates peace treaty with Mithridates I; establishes himself as dictator in Rome
71 BC Pompeius Magnus, Roman general, suppresses a two year-long slave revolt led by gladiator Spartacus
70-19 BC Life of Virgil, Roman poet and author of the poem *Aeneid*

'I fear the Greeks, even if they carry presents'
VIRGIL

70 BC Crassus and Pompeius Magnus elected as Consuls of Rome
66 BC Pompeius Magnus defeats King Mithridates VI of Pontus (Turk.)
65 BC- 8 AD Life of Horace, Roman lyric poet, famous for his poem *Carmina*
60 BC 'First Triumvirate' Julius Caesar, Pompeius Magnus and Marcus Crassus, rule Rome

Roman Rule

58-52 BC 'Gallic Wars' Julius Caesar, Roman general, invades Gaul (France, Belgium, The Netherlands, up to the river Rhine)
57 BC Julius Caesar describes Gallia Belgica as northern Gaul, between the rivers Meuse (Bel.), Marne (Fr.) and Seine (Fr.)

'Of all the Gauls, the Belgae are the bravest, being farthest from the developed civilisation of Rome and closest to the Germanic people, because merchants least frequently resort to them, and import those things which tend to effeminate the mind'
COMMENTARII DE BELLO GALLICO, CAESAR

55 BC Romans invade Britain
52 BC 'Battle of Alesia (Fr.)' Vercingetorix, Chieftain of the Gauls, surrenders to Romans under Julius Caesar; last phase of the Gallic wars

49 BC Julius Caesar departs from his designated province Gaul and crosses the boundary river Rubicon (Ravenna, It.) with his legion; violating Roman law and provoking a civil war, which he wins

'Alea iacta est!'

'*The die is cast!*', CAESAR CRIES, CROSSING THE RUBICON

48 BC Senate elects Julius Caesar as Consul; Pompeius Magnus killed on his way to Egypt

47 BC Romans reach the Rhine, northern 'limes' (border) of the Roman Empire; build fortifications at Maastricht (N. Lim.) and Nijmegen (N. Bra.)

47 BC Julius Caesar defeats King Ptolemy XIII of Egypt; Julius Caesar installs Cleopatra on the throne, together with her brother Ptolemy XIV

47 BC 'Battle of Zela (Turk.)' Julius Caesar annihilates King Pharnaces II of Pontus

'Veni, vidi, vici.'

'*I came, I saw, I conquered.*', REPORTS CAESAR AFTER HIS RETURN TO ROME

44 BC Julius Caesar announces expedition to the Partians; on the Ides (15th) of March many senators, among them Marcus Brutus, participate in murdering him in the Senate

'Et tu, Brute?'

'*You too, Brutus?*', EXCLAIMS CAESAR, WHEN BRUTUS ATTACKS HIM

43-27 BC 'Second Triumvirate' under Gauis Octavian, nephew and posthumously adopted son of Julius Caesar; keeps the power of the Roman Empire in the west and leaves the east to Mark Antony

37 BC Mark Antony invites Cleopatra to the eastern Roman capital Antioch (Syria)

31 BC 'Sea battle near Actium (Gr.)' between fleets of Octavian and Mark Antony & Cleopatra; Octavian wins a decisive victory, occupies Alexandria (Egyp.) and makes Egypt a Roman province

31 BC-14 AD Octavian rules as the first Emperor of Rome

30 BC Mark Antony and Cleopatra commit suicide

27 BC Senate awards Octavian the honorific title of Augustus

c 3 BC Birth of Jesus of Nazareth

9 AD 'Battle of the Teutoburg Forest' Germanic tribes defeat the Roman Army; the Rhine remains the border-river of the Roman Empire

15 Gallica Belgica becomes a Roman province

25-100 Direct sea trade between Rome and India

26-36 Pontius Pilate governs the Roman province of Judea (Isr.)

28 Romans give up the province of Friesland, after an uprising

'Famous was from then on, the name of the Frisians under the Germanic tribes'
TACITUS

33 Jesus of Nazareth crucified

'Father, forgive them; for they know not what they do'
LUKE'S GOSPEL, THE BIBLE

43 London founded by the Romans

47 Romans dig *Canal of Corbulo,* now de Vliet (S. Hol.); links the Meuse and the Rhine, which permits safe journey behind the dunes instead of by sea

c 50 Navigators from Indonesia colonise Madagascar (Ind. Oc.)

c 50 Kushans from Persia penetrate into India

c 55-120 Life of Publius Tacitus, Roman historian, who writes 'sine ira et studio' (without either anger or zeal)
64 Emperor Nero persecutes Christians; Rome set on fire

69-70 Uprising of Cananefaten and Batavians under Julius Civilus against Romans; ends in their defeat
70-270 *Pax Romana* Prosperity and romanisation south of the Rhine; beginnings of literacy

79 Eruption of Mount Vesuvius; destroys Pompeii and Herculaneum near Naples (It.)
80 Colosseum of Rome completed
c 100 Buddhism reaches China; by 450 about 90% of its population is Buddhist
c 105 Chinese invent paper-making
117-138 Emperor Hadrian erected *Hadrian's Wall* to protect Roman Britain against invasions from the north
135 Romans defeat a Jewish uprising and destroy the *Temple of Jerusalem*; beginning of Jewish diaspora
138-161 Emperor Antoine built *Antonine Wall* 75 miles north of *Hadrian's Wall*

Germanic Tribes

161-180 Emperor Marcus: Aurelius resists invasion of Germanic Tribes; writes his famous work *Meditations,* a work of Stoic philosophy

'It is always for the same reasons that the Germanic tribes came over to Gallia: lust, greed, wanting to move! They want to quit their moors and wilderness to steal your fertile land and yourself.'

TACITUS

Low Countries

c 200 Germanic peoples form alliances

c 250-400 Roman dominance disappears under pressure from the Goths

259-268 Batavian Regent Marcus Postumus usurps power and forms the Gallic Empire with its capital in Cologne (Ger.)

c 300 First propagation of the Gospel in the Low Countries

Wider World

180-284 'Crisis of the Third Century' Period in which the Roman Empire nearly collapses under the pressures of invasion, civil war, the Plague and economic depression; Roman Emperors are usually cruel and perverse

211 Emperor Septimus Severus dies in York (Eng.); first Roman Emperor for eighty years not to die a violent death
224-651 Sassanid dynasty rules Persia; cultural and scientific revival
220-581 'Era of Disunity' dominates China

251 Goths defeat the Roman Emperor Decius
256 Persians use poison gas (pitch and sulphur) against Romans, along the river Euphrates (Syria)

275-276 Devastation in Gaul by Franks and Alamanni, both Germanic tribes
286 Emperor Diocletian splits the Roman Empire; retains the eastern part and appoints Maximian as his successor in the western part

c 300 Chinese invent the stirrup; allows the horseman a better hold
300-400 Buddhism spreads across South East Asia
300-900 Maya culture in Central America; noted for its written language as well as for its art, architecture and mathematical systems
301 King Tiridates III makes Armenia the first country with Christianity as state religion

Low Countries

Wider World

305 Diocletian resigns voluntarily as Emperor of Rome together with his co-emperor Maximian
306-333 Constantine I (the Great), first Christian Emperor of Rome
313 'Edict of Milan' Constantine the Great decrees religious toleration in the Roman Empire
320-520 Gupta dynasty rules India
325 *Council of Nicaea* (Turk.) results in first statement of Christian doctrine
330 Constantine the Great transforms the Greek colony of Byzantium on the river Bosporus (Turk.) into the capital of the East Roman Empire; remains its capital for over thousand years
337 Death of Constantine the Great; Byzantium renamed Constantinople

346-384 St Servatius, Bishop of Tongeren (Fl. Lim.) and Maastricht (N. Lim.)

350-374 Ermanaric, King of the Goths, establishes his realm between the Black Sea and the Finnish Gulf
354-430 Life of St Augustine, romanised Berber philosopher, writes inter alia *Confessions*
366-562 Japanese rule Korea
370-568 'The Great Migration' Huns, nomadic people from beyond river Volga (Rus.), migrate and build up an empire in Europe; drive Goths from Central Europe, who in turn force Germanic peoples into the Roman Empire
406 Germanic tribes invade the Campine (Fl. Bra.) and Land of Waas (E. Flan.)
372 Huns defeat Ostrogoths near river Don (Rus.)
c 375 Japanese adopt writing with Chinese characters
376 Fleeing Visigoths, a Germanic people, find shelter in the Roman Empire
c 400 Christianity reaches Ireland

406 Germanic tribes invade the Campine (Fl. Bra.) and Land of Waas (E. Flan.)

406 Vandals, an East Germanic tribe, cross the river Rhine; beginning the invasion of Gaul
406-453 Life of Attila, leader of the Hunnish Empire, which stretches from Germany to the Ural mountains (Rus.) and from the Danube river to the Baltic sea
409-428 Vandals cross Pyrenees and settle in Spain
410 Visigoths sack Rome
411 Pelagius, ascetic monk from the British Isles, denies the doctrine of original sin
415-456 King Kumaragupta of the Gupta dynasty rules India; establishes the then largest university of Asia in Nalanda, now Bihar (India)
418 Visigoths occupy southern France and Spain; pushing Vandals into northern Africa
439 Vandals conquer Carthage

Merovingian Period

450 Chlodio (the Hairy), King of the Franks, makes Tournai (Hain.) the centre of the Merovingian realm; fills the power vacuum left by Romans

c 450 Slavs invade and settle in the Balkans
From 450 Angles, Saxons and Jutes from Germany invade England; Celtic Brits cross to Brittany (Fr.)
451 'The Battle of Chalon (Fr.)' Romans, Visigoths and Franks defeat Huns and Ostrogoths, who retreat over the Rhine; leaving fifteen thousand dead on the Catalaunian Fields
455 Vandals sack Rome
460-528 Huns invade North India
476 Odoacer, leader of Germanic settlers, deposes Romulus Augustus, the last Emperor of the West Roman Empire

Dark Ages

481-511 Clovis I, King of the Franks, makes Paris capital of Merovingian realm; leads to the rise of two languages (French from Latin and Dutch from German)

480-543 Life of St Benedict of Nursia, Italian hermit, who lays down rules for monastic life in western Europe

488 King Theodoric leads Ostrogoths from Danube region to establish Ostrogoth Kingdom in Italy

496 Clovis I converts to Christianity; fundamental step for northwest Europe

c 500 Hinduism reaches Indonesia

507 Clovis I defeats Visigoths; rules over whole of Gaul

527-565 Justinian I (the Great), Eastern Roman Emperor, conquers large part of northern Africa and Italy; codifies all Roman law into one *Corpus Juris Civilis*

529 St Benedict of Nursia founds monastery of Monte Cassino (It.)

531-579 King Chosroes I of Persia conquers Egypt; Persian Empire reaches its largest size

532-536 *Hagia Sophia* (Holy Wisdom), Cathedral of Constantinople, rebuilt after a fire

541-542 Plague strikes Constantinople; a quarter of the population dies

552 East Roman Empire retakes Rome from the Ostrogoths

552-967 Khazars, semi-nomadic Turkish people, peacefully dominate the Steppe north of the Black Sea; stimulate trade with eastern Europe

562 Avars, a nomadic Turkish tribe from the Steppe, invade the Balkans

568 Lombards occupy northern Italy, reducing East Roman influence there; Slavs fill the vacuum in the East Roman Empire

570-620 State of Tibet is founded
575 Mathematicians from India use decimal fractions and the number zero from China
581-618 Sui dynasty unifies China; Chang'an (now Xi'an) becomes its capital
590-604 Pope Gregory I establishes the Papal States in Italy
593-622 Prince Shotoku, member of the Soga dynasy, creates one central Japanese state
c 600 Maya civilisation reaches its summit
From 600 Latin sails come into use in European waters; enable ships to cruise against the wind, which is not possible with cross-rigged sails

600-850 Frisians trade from Dorestad (Utr.) with northern Europe

610 Emperor Heraclius accedes to the throne of the Byzantine Empire; introduces Greek as the Empire's official language
616 Visigoths remove Byzantines from southern Spain
618-907 Tang dynasty assumes power in China; *Silk Roads* to Arabia and Europe further developed
622 Muhammad, Arab prophet and founder of the religion of Islam, starts to preach the Koran; beginning of the Islamic calendar
622-623 Serbs, Slavic people, retreat from northern Germany to the Balkans; lay foundations of Croatia and Serbia

629-639 Reign of Dagobert I, King of the Franks; Pepin I (the Elder) acts as his Major Domus (Mayor of the Palace)

632-710 Arabian Caliphs conquer Persia and its remaining parts of the Middle East and northern Africa
634-644 Omar (Commander of the Faithful), the second Caliph of the Arab realm

635-714 Pepin II (the Younger), Major Domus of the Frank realm; makes the function of Major Domus hereditary
647 St Amand, French Christian saint, Bishop of Maastricht (N. Lim.) and Tongeren (Fl. Lim.)

649 Arabs conquer the island of Cyprus (Gr. / Turk.)
c 650 Bulgarians settle north of the river Danube
650-750 Islamic faith spreads by means of the Arab trade routes from
Spain to Indonesia; one religion, one culture and one law unite the trade of the world for nearly one thousand years
650-1250 Kingdom of Champa established in present Vietnam and Cambodia
655 'Battle of the Masts' Muslim Arabs fleet defeats Byzantine fleet near Dhat Al-Sawari (Turk.); Arabs secure the sea route to India and China for nearly one thousand years

658-739 Life of St Willibrord, English missionary; brings Christianity to the Frisians

659 Chinese Kingdom extends into Central Asia
661-750 Omayyad dynasty rules the Arab realm from its capital Damascus (Syria)
672-678 Arabs unsuccessfully attack Constantinople

689 'Battle near Dorestad (Utr.)' Pepin II defeats Frisians
696 Diocese of Utrecht established; St Willibrord consecrated Bishop of the Frisians

697-1797 Venetian City-Republic exists under guidance of one hundred and seventeen successive Doges for eleven centuries
From 700 Kingdom of Ghana emerges in western Africa

700-1200 Islamic states in Asia, Africa and Europe surpass Christian states in culture and science *Pax Islamica*

705 St Lambert, Bishop of Maastricht (N. Lim.), the first Saint from the Low Countries is murdered near Liège

711 Tariq ibn Ziyad, former Berber slave, defeats Visigoths near Jabil Tariq (Gibraltar) and occupies Spain; liberates local Jews from Visigoth yoke

716-754 St Boniface, English missionary, propagates Christianity in Frankish Empire

Carolingian Period

717-741 Charles Martel, Major Domus, founder of the Carolingian dynasty, rules the Frankish Kingdom

730-787 'Byzantine Iconoclasm' causes rift between East Orthodox Church and Roman Catholic Church

732 'Battle of Tours (Fr.)' Charles Martel defeats the Umayyad Caliphate Army; prevents further Islamisation of western Europe

734 'Battle of river Boorne (Frl.)' Charles Martel defeats Frisians; end of Frisian independence

750 Lombards conquer Ravenna (It.); end of Byzantine power in Central Italy

750-1258 'Abbasid Caliphate' Al-Saffah (the Slaughterer) overthrows Marwan II, the last Umayyad Caliph and rules from Baghdad (Iraq); his realm stretches from North Africa to Persia and India; Baghdad develops into centre of international trade and culture

751 Pippin III (the Short), King of the Franks, elected by Frankish nobility

751 'Battle of Talas (Kyrgyz.)' Abbasid Caliphate Army defeats the Chinese Tang Army for control of the river Syr Darya (Uzbek.); Chinese expansionism versus Arab expansionism

754 St Boniface murdered near Dokkum (Frl.)

755-795 Tibetan King Trisong Detsen expands his empire into Nepal, northern Pakistan, Turkistan and parts of northern India and western China

756-1013 'Umayyad Emirate of Al-Andalus (Córdoba, Sp.)' founded by exiled Umayyad Prince Abd ar-Rahman I, rules Iberian Peninsula and part of North Africa; remarkable success in trade and culture

768-814 Charlemagne (the Great) succeeds Pepin the Short as King of the Franks and expands his realm into Germany and Italy

774 Charlemagne defeats Lombards in Italy; southern Italy remains in Byzantine hands

779 Charlemagne standardises the coinage (1 pound = 20 shillings = 240 pence)

785 Charlemagne forces the Saxons to convert to Christianity

786-809 Reign of Caliph Harun al-Rashid (the Upright); stimulates culture and science in the Arab realm

788 Construction of the Great Mosque of Córdoba (Sp.) starts

791-797 Charlemagne the Great inflicts heavy losses on Avars, a pagan Asian horde, settled in Hungary

793-1000 Vikings from Scandinavia invade the coasts of Europe, up to the Black Sea

794 Emperor Kammu moves capital of Japan to Kyoto; start of classical Heian period

Low Countries

800 Pope Leo III crowns Charlemagne Emperor of the Holy Roman Empire; Franks, Frisians and Saxons become part of the Carolingian realm, which results in conflicting civilisations

From 800 Feudal system becomes widespread

814-840 Louis I (the Pious), King of the Franks, succeeds Charlemagne

835 Vikings conquer Dorestad (now Wijk bij Duurstede, Utr.); at that time the largest city in the Low Countries

840 Death of Louis the Pious; his three sons plunge into a civil war for the inheritance

Middle Francia / West Francia

843 'Treaty of Verdun' divides the Carolingian Empire into three parts; East Francia to Louis (the German), Middle Francia with the northern Low Countries, Luxembourg, Alsace, Lorraine, Burgundy, Provence and Italy to Lothair I and West Francia and Flanders to Charles II (the Bald)

Wider World

c 800 Construction of Buddhist monument *Borobudur* in Central Java (Indon.)

827 Arabs conquer the island of Crete (Gr.)

c 836 Vikings start ravaging the English coast

840 Kyrgyz defeat Uyghurs in the Yenisey delta (Siberia); end of Uyghur Khaganate

846 Arabs ransack Vatican and Rome

862 Rurik I, Viking Chieftain and founder of Rurik dynasty builds settlement near Novgorod (Rus.)

c 868 *Diamond Sutra* (Diamond Rules), first block printed book, contains Buddhist canon

870 Arabs conquer the island of Malta

c 870 Chinese invent gunpowder

Low Countries | Wider World

875 Charles the Bald, conquers Italy; Emperor of the Holy Roman Empire

882 Godfried the Sea King and his Vikings plunder Deventer (Ove.) and Zutphen (Gel.)

882 Vikings destroy the city of Trier (Ger.)
882 Rurik I makes Kiev (Rus.) capital of the Kievian Rus state
886 Vikings lay siege to Paris

888-1428 Brabant, Flanders and Holland exist as quasi independent principalities; owing formal allegiance to the French or the German King
898-922 Charles III (the Simple), King of Germany and Holy Roman Emperor, temporarily unites the three parts of the Carolingian Empire (France, Germany and Italy)

899-945 Magyars invade eastern Europe; settle in Hungary

From 900 Prosperity in Brabant and Flanders increases

900-1000 Maori colonise Aotearoa (New Zeal.)

900-1400 Feudal system stimulates development of class society

907-960 'Period of Five Dynasties and Ten Kingdoms' Era of political upheaval in China
909-1171 Fatimid Caliphate moves to Tunis, conquers Egypt and Syria; makes Cairo its capital
910 Benedictine Abbey founded at Cluny (Fr.)
911 Charles the Simple cedes Normandy as a fief to Rollo the Norman, the first Duke of Normandy; Charles' daughter becomes Rollo's wife
919-936 Henry I (the Fowler), King of Germany, founds Saxon dynasty; ends Carolingian rule in Germany

925 Henry the Fowler annexes Lotharingia; northern Low Countries fall under German rule, Flanders remains a fief of the King of France

933 City of Delhi founded in India
939 General Ngo Quen gains freedom for Vietnam, after 1000 years of Chinese occupation; Dai Co Viet Kingdom founded
955 'Battle of Lechveld (Ger.)' Emperor Otto I of Germany defeats the Magyars; halting their westward expansion
960-1126 Northern Song dynasty controls most of China proper; issues paper money and establishes a permanent standing navy
965 Arabs conquer Sicily
971-1018 Byzantines subdue Bulgarians
986 Vikings reach Greenland (Atl. Ocean)
987 Hugh Capet, French nobleman, elected King of France
992 Byzantium and Venice conclude a trade treaty
997-1038 Stephan I (the Holy), first King of Hungary
c 1000 Romani (Gypsies) migrate from Rasjashan (Ind.) via the island of Corfu (Gr.) to the Balkans
c 1000 1000 King Svjatoslav of Kiev defeats Khazars and conquers the Balkans; conversion to the East Orthodox faith

1000-1385 Feudal Lords in the Low Countries strive for independence from their sovereigns

1014 Aethelred (the Unready) returns as King after England has endured years of raids by Vikings
1016-1035 Viking King Cnut II (the Great), rules England, Denmark and Norway
1027 Vikings arrive in southern Italy
1030 Avicenna (Ibn Sina), polymath of Persian origin, compiles the first medical encyclopaedia, *The Canon of Medicine*

1044-1077 King Anawrahta founds Burma with Pagan as capital
1054 Schism between Roman Catholic and Orthodox Christian Churches
1055 Seljuk Turks under Sultan Toghrul capture Baghdad (Iraq); setting up of Abbasid Caliphate
1061 Vikings land on Sicily
1065 Westminster Abbey in London completed
1066 'Battle of Hastings (Eng.)' William (the Conqueror), Duke of Normandy, lands near Hastings; defeats Anglo-Saxons and becomes King of England
1074 *Bayeux Tapestry* Embroidered cloth depicts the Norman conquest of England
1075 Seljuk Turks conquer Jerusalem from Fatimid Caliphate
1075-1122 'Investiture Controversy' Conflict among German Emperors and Popes over control of church officials; controversy leads to 50 years of civil war in Germany
1075-1500 In connection with the Investure Controversy, Guelphs (Dukes of Bavaria) and Ghibellines (Kings of Sicily) respectively support the Papacy and the Holy Roman Empire in Italy; division persists into the 15th century
1076 Vikings discover Vinland, now Newfoundland (Can.)
1077 *Walk to Canossa* King Henry IV of Germany does penance to reverse excommunication by Pope Gregory VII; changes relationship between church and state
1085 Alfonso VI (el Bravo), King of Spain, chases the Arabs out of Toledo (Sp.); beginning of the *Reconquista* (Recapture) of Spain
1086 *The Domesday Book* Survey of all English dwellings and possessions to determine taxation

'There was no single hide nor indeed was one ox, one cow or one pig not put down in this record'
DOMESDAY BOOK

1090 Norman Count Roger I of Sicily, conquers Malta
1094 Rodrigo de Vivar (El Cid, the Master), Castilian nobleman, conquers Valencia (Sp.) from Arabs
1095 Pope Urban II calls for a crusade to wrestle the Holy Land from the Seljuk Turks
1096-1099 Christian soldiers under Godfrey of Bouillon, Duke of Lower Lorraine, take Jerusalem after bloody siege; Christians become acquainted with Arab culture and Greek philosophy
1099 Sovereign Military Hospitaller Order of St John (the Knights of Malta) founded in Jerusalem

From 1100 Reclaiming the marshes; stimulates the democratic process among the farmers
From 1100 Flemish cities of Antwerp, Bruges, Ghent and Ypres grow powerful; municipal rights laid down in by-laws
c 1100 The oldest known phrase in the Dutch language

'Hebban olla vogala nestas hagunnan hinase, hic anda thu, wat unbidan we nu?'
'All birds have started their nests, except you and me, what are we waiting for?'

1116 University of Bologna (It.) founded
1118 Knights Templar, a mainly military order, founded
1119 Magnetised needle for navigational purposes, i.e. compass, used in China
1122 'Concordat of Worms' German Emperor Henry V loses control over the church; de facto separation between church and state

1127-1279 Southern Song dynasty rules southern China; after losing northern China (Manchuria) to the Yin dynasty
1128 Portugal independent from the Kingdom of León (Sp.)
1135 Flying buttresses used in construction of French Gothic churches
c 1140 Construction of *Angkor Wat*, Hindu temple complex in Cambodia built for the Khmer King Suryavarman II; largest religious complex on earth
c 1140 'Mazarabs' Christians living under Muslim rule in al-Andaluz (Sp.) forced to retreat from there; spread the Arabic figures and the abacus (Chinese counting device) in western Europe, which facilitates trade
1147-1149 'Second Crusade' Siege of Damascus fails
1155 Adrian IV, only Englishman to become Pope, gives King Henry II of England lordship over Ireland
1155-1190 Frederick I (Barbarossa), King of Germany and Italy, Holy Roman Emperor, founder of the Hohenstaufen dynasty; after his reign, German unity crumbles
1158 Emperor Frederick I destroys Milan; Italy remains in revolt
1163 First stone of Parisian Gothic Cathedral of Notre Dame laid

c 1170 First known vernacular Flemish writer Hendrik van Veldeke publishes *Legend of St Servaas*

1172-1195 *Giralda* Minaret measuring 105 metres, built in Seville (Sp.)
1174 Construction of the *Tower of Pisa* (It.) starts
1187 Saladin, Sultan of Egypt and Syria, captures Jerusalem; but spares the civil population

1189-1192 'Third Crusade' Richard I (the Lionheart) King of England, fails to retake Jerusalem; conquers Cyprus instead

1189 'Teutonic Knights' German Roman Catholic religious order establishes hospitals to treat wounded crusaders

1192 Minamoto no Yoromito receives the title of Shogun (military leader), shares power with Emperor; establishes the first Shogunate in Japan

1194 Henry VI, Holy Roman Emperor, defeats the local Arabs and conquers Sicily

1194 Construction of *Cathedral of Chartres* (Fr.) begins

1200 University of Paris founded

c 1200 Inca capital Cuzco founded in Peru

From 1200 Water Boards, governmental bodies, regulate the water levels in reclaimed marshes; the oldest democratic institutions in the Low Countries

1200-1380 Republic of Venice dominates the Mediterranean Sea

1200-1400 Social unrest between patricians and plebeians in Flemish cities

1200-1500 Italian merchants from Venice and Genoa ship slaves (Mameluks) from Caucasus (Rus./Georg.) to Egypt and the Levant (Lebanon) for service in local armies

1202-1204 Pope Innocent III calls for the Fourth Crusade, Crusaders conquer and sack Constantinople; widens the schism between Greek Orthodox Church and Roman Catholic Church

1204 Count Baldwin of Flanders crowned Emperor of Constantinople; Venice conquers the island of Crete

1206-1227 Rule of Genghis Khan, founder of the Mongol Empire; largest contiguous Empire in history

1206-1526 Several Turkish and Afghan dynasties rule the Delhi Sultanate (India)

1209-1226 'Albigensian Crusade' against the Cathars (religious party which rejects the Old Testament); results in the annexation of Languedoc by France
1210-1310 Knights of Malta rule Cyprus
1212-1645 Crete remains under rule of Venice
1215 *Magna Carta* (Legal Charter) Document signed by English King John under pressure from his subjects; leads to constitutional law

'To no man will we sell, or deny or delay right or justice'
MAGNA CHARTA

1216 St Dominic, Spanish monk, founds the Order of Friar Preachers (Dominicans)

1218-1221 'Fifth Crusade' Participating Dutch, Flemish and Frisian soldiers under Count William I of Holland, play a major role; but the crusade fails after intervention by Pope Honorius III
1220 Count William I of Holland grants municipal rights to Dordrecht (S. Hol.)

1220 Genghis Khan conquers Samarkand (Uzbek.)
1220-1250 Rule of Frederick II, King of Sicily, Holy Roman Emperor, Stupor Mundi (Wonder of the World), said to speak six languages; suppresses revolt of Muslims on Sicily
1222 University of Padua (It.) founded
1224 Genghis Khan leads the Mongols into Europe

1227 'Battle of the river Ane' Farmers from the province of Drenthe defeat the knights' army of the Bishop of Utrecht; first uprising against a feudal lord in the Low Countries

1230 Kingdom of León (Sp.) united with the Kingdom of Castile (Sp.) under King Ferdinand III
1232 First military use of rockets in China

1234-1256 Rule of William II, Count of Holland, and from 1248 Holy Roman Emperor; founder of The Hague

c 1235 Rise of the Kingdom of Mali (W. Africa) under Mansa Musa
1237-1241 Mongols penetrate into eastern Europe
1239-1358 Tibet is a vassal state of the Mongol Yuan dynasty in China
1240-1480 Rule of Kipchak-khanat (Golden Horde); Russian Steppe under the yoke of Mongol-Turkish rule
1241 Hungarian city of Boeda demolished by Mongols
1248 King Ferdinand III of Castile recaptures Seville (Sp.) from the Arabs
1249 University of Oxford (Eng.) founded
c 1250 Muslim Arabs conquer Sumatra (Indon.)

c 1250 Willem van Boudelo, Flemish Cistercian monk, writes an allegorical fable *Reynard the Fox*

c 1250 Portuguese chase the Moors from their country; two hundred years before the Spanish do the same
c 1250 Ibn al-Nafis, Arab scholar, describes the pulmonary circulation of the blood through the lungs
1250 Invasion of Egypt by King Louis IX of France fails
1250-1273 'Great Interregnum'
Frederick II, last Holy Roman Emperor of the Hohenstaufen dynasty, dies without successor; after a period of political chaos, the Empire passes to the Habsburg dynasty
1250-1570 Mameluk dynasty rules Egypt

1251 City of Ghent (E-Fla.) connected by canal to the Zwin, a tidal inlet of the North Sea

1253-1299 Series of naval wars rage between Genoa and Venice

1254 William of Rubruc, Flemish Franciscan missionary and explorer, visits Karakorum (Mong.), capital of the Mongol Empire

1258 Mongols overrun Baghdad (Iraq), leading centre of Islamic culture
1259-1294 Rule of Kublai Khan, grandson of Genghis Kahn, Great Khan of the Mongol Empire; *Pax Mongolia*
1260 'Battle of Ain Jalut (Isr.)' Egyptian Mameluks defeat Mongols; ends the height of Mongol conquests
1267 *Hanseatic League* Economic alliance of trading cities and their guilds around the Baltic Sea, founded in Lübeck (Ger.)
1267 St Thomas Aquinas, Italian Dominican theologian, writes *Summa Theologica*
1271-1291 Marco Polo, Italian explorer, visits China, India and Mongolia
1271-1368 Yuan dynasty founded by the Mongol Emperor Kublai Khan, rules China, Mongolia and Tibet; continuation of the Mongol Empire and Imperial dynasty of China
1273 Rudolph I of Germany and Holy Roman Emperor, defeats Ottokar II, King of Bohemia; establishes the Habsburg dynasty in Austria
1274-1281 Failed Mongol invasions under Kublai Khan into Japan; the only threat in history to Japan, until World War II
1277-1395 Visconti dynasty rules Milan (It.)
1281 Cambridge (Eng.) University founded
1284 Republic of Venice mints the first gold coin *Ducat*
1287 Mongols plunder Pagan, capital of Burma
1288-1919 Ottoman dynasty rules Turkey
1291 Republic of Genoa conquers Muslim ruled Gibraltar (Sp.)

1291 Mameluks take the city of Akko (Isr.); foothold of the Crusaders

1291 Swiss Confederation formed by the cantons Unterwalden, Uri and Schwyz

1294 Pope Boniface VIII succeeds Pope Celestine V, the only Pope who abdicates; an era of cases of immorality of the Popes ends

1294-1312 Rule of Duke John II of Brabant, the first ruler in Europe who allows the estates to participate by the 'Charter of Kortenberg'

1296 Floris V (God of the common people), Count of Holland, murdered near Muiden (N. Hol.)

c 1300 Gunpowder from China reaches Europe

From 1300 Cities in the northern Low Countries: Delft, Dordrecht, Haarlem and Leyden grow; rise of the burghers (third estate)

1300-1500 Guilds of rhetoric enliven the Low Countries with songs and plays

1302 'Battle of the Spurs' Flemish foot soldiers defeat French knights near Kortrijk (W. Flan.); confirms Flemish independence

1305 Giotto, Italian painter and architect, makes frescoes in the Santa Maria Chapel in Padua (It.)

1307 Alighieri Dante, Italian poet and politician, starts his epic poem *La Divina Commedia* (The Divine Comedy) in three parts: Inferno, Purgatorio and Paradiso

1309-1376 Popes exchange Rome, seat of the Catholic Church, for Avignon (Fr.); under French pressure

1312 Count Henry VII of Luxembourg, King of Bohemia, crowned as Holy Roman Emperor in Rome, but outside St Peter's Basilica

1312 Pope Clements V dissolves the Knights Templar; their possessions are transferred to the Order of St John
1325-1351 Sultan Muhammad Ibn Tughluq of Delhi gives his realm its largest extension in North and Central India; maintains the sharia (Islamite religious law) with force
1325-1519 Aztec (Mesoamericans) civilisation dominates Mexico
1331 Plague ravages China; its population diminishes by about 30%
1331-1335 Serbian Tsar Stephan Dushan rules over the Balkans
1334 Giotto, Italian architect and painter, designs the *Campanile* (tower) in Florence (It.)
1337-1453 'Hundred Years' War' fought by England and France for the French throne in France and the Low Countries; House of Valois established as the ruling dynasty

1338 Revolutionary rule to break the English blockade of wool and food supply in Flanders by Jacob van Arteveld, a Flemish merchant
1340 'Battle of Sluys (Zee.)' fought between naval fleets of England and France; won by the English with help from Flemish ships
1345 "Battle of Warns (Frl.)' Count William IV of Holland, Zeeland and Hainaut, slain by the Frisians led by Great Peter

'Leaver dea as slaef'
'Better dead, than a slave' MOTTO OF GREAT PETER

1345-1428 'Hook and Cod Wars' fought over the title of Count of Holland

1346 Plague comes via the Silk Route into Kaffa (Feodosiya, Crimea); drives the Mongols from Europe

1347 Plague arrives in Constantinople and Messina (Sicily); leads to decline of Islamic rule

1348 Charles IV, Holy Roman Emperor, founds the first university of his realm in the capital of Prague

1348-1350 Plague spreads throughout Europe; the population declines by 30-60%

c 1350 Gutting and curing of herrings developed by Dutch Willem Beukelszoon of Biervliet (Zee.)

1350-1550 Bruges (W. Flan.), Deventer (Ove.), Ghent (E. Flan.), Zwolle (Ove.) participate with other cities in the Hanseatic League

1355 'Battle of Ihtiman (Bul.)' Ottoman Turks invade Europe and defeat the Bulgarian Army

1358-1720 Dalai Lama govern Tibet theocratically with support of their rulers in China

Burgundian Netherlands

1363-1404 Rule of Philip II (the Bold), Duke of Burgundy; conquers Flanders, Artois (Fr.) and Franche-Comté (Fr.) in 1384

1365 City of Alexandria (Egyp.) sacked by Crusaders under King Peter of Cyprus and knights of the Order of St John; the most humiliating Crusade

1366 Francesco Petrarca, Italian poet and founding father of humanism, writes *Canzoniere* (Sonnets for Laura)

1368-1644 Ming dynasty replaces the Mongol Yuan dynasty, weakened by the Plague; era of orderly government and social stability, repair of the Chinese Wall

1370-1405 Turkish-Mongol ruler Tamerlane (the Lame), conquers Samarkand, Central Asia, northern India, Iraq, Iran, Syria and eastern Turkey; dies whilst invading China

1378-1417 'Papal Schism' Two men, one in Avignon (Fr.) and one in Rome (It.) both claim to be the true Pope; hurts the reputation of the office

1385 Portugal, under rule of King John I and Queen Philippa of Lancaster, becomes independent from Spain; long-lasting alliance between England and Portugal develops

1385 'Double Marriage' John (the Fearless), Duke of Burgundy, marries Magaretha of Bavaria and William II, Duke of Bavaria, marries Magaretha of Burgundy; joins the Bavarian House with the Burgundian House, which rules over Artois (Fr.), Mechlin (Antw.) and Flanders

1385 'Peace of Tournai (Hain.)' Settlement between Philip the Bold and the city of Ghent (E. Flan.); French king to be recognised, city rights preserved

1386 Philip the Bold sets up Council Chambers in Dijon (Fr.) and Lille (Fr.)

1387 Geoffrey Chaucer, English poet, writes his magnum opus, the collection of stories *Canterbury Tales*

1389 'Battle of Kosovo' Ottoman Turks defeat the Serb Army near Prestina (Kosovo); Serbia becomes a vassal state to the Ottomans

1393 Ottoman Turks occupy Bulgaria

1393-1449 Life of Ulugh Beg, Persian astronomer and ruler of Transoxiana (Uzbek.); builds an observatory in Samarkand (Uzbek.)

1394-1460 Life of Prince Henry of Portugal (the Navigator); stimulates beginning of European worldwide explorations

1397-1523 'Kalmar Union' unites the Kingdoms of Denmark, Norway and Sweden under one ruler, Queen Margaret of Denmark

Renaissance

From 1400 Renaissance (revival of art and science) starts in Italy; influences western and central Europe

1400-1585 Economic centre of the western world moves from Bruges (W. Flan.) to Antwerp (Antw.)
1404-1419 Reign of John the Fearless, Duke of Burgundy
1405 *The Council of Flanders* John the Fearless installs a Court of Justice

1405-1433 Admiral Tsjeng He leads seven Chinese expeditions with up to 300 ships, measuring up to 100 metres to the eastern African coast; Tsjeng conquers Ceylon
1408 Donatello, Italian sculptor, creates *David*
1410-1737 The Medici banking family and Maecenas's, hold power in Florence (It.); family counts three Popes and two Queens
1411-1414 Chinese Admiral Yishiha explores the river Amur (border between China and Siberia)
1415 Portuguese conquer their first colony, Ceuta (Moroc.)
1415 John Hus, Czech scholar and forerunner of the Reformation, burnt at the stake in Konstanz (Ger.); twenty years of revolts by the Hussites in Bohemia (Czech.)

1418 Jacoba of Bavaria, Countess of Hainaut, Holland and Zeeland, marries her cousin John IV, Duke of Brabant

1419-1467 Reign of Philip III (the Good), Duke of Burgundy, first conquers Hainaut (Fr.), Holland, Luxembourg, Namur and Zeeland and later on conquers Brabant and Limburg, plus gaining the protectorate over the Bishopric Principality of Liège; lays the basis for a nation in the Low Countries

c 1420 Jamshid Kashani, Persian astronomer and mathematician, uses decimal fractions and the number zero

1421 *St Elizabeth Flood* inundates parts of Holland, Flanders and Zeeland; killing ten thousand people

1425 University of Leuven (Fl. Bra.) founded

1428 'Reconciliation of Delft (S. Hol.)' Jacoba of Bavaria and Philip the Good terminate the Hook and Cod Wars; Jacoba of Bavaria transfers her rights to Philip the Good

1430 'Maid of Orleans' Joan of Arc, French religious peasant girl, leads the French Army; burnt at the stake by the English in Rouen (Fr.)

c 1430 Jan van Eyck, Flemish artist from Maaseik (N. Lim.) uses oil paint; refines the art of painting

1432-1481 Life of Mehmet II (the Conqueror), Ottoman Sultan; extends the Islamic Empire with Egypt, Greece, Asia Minor, Mesopotamia and Palestine

1435 Leon Battista Alberti, Italian humanist, describes the linear perspective for the first time in *De pictura* (about painting)

1435 King Charles VII of France releases Philip the Good from his feudal obligations

1436 French capture Paris from the English

1438-1806 Habsburg Princes hold the title of German Emperor; build up their influence from Austria
1438 Inca Empire established from present Ecuador to Chile
1440 Eton (Eng.) College founded
1443-1490 Life of Matthias Corvinus, King of Hungary, King of Bohemia and Duke of Austria; unites Hungary with Bohemia
1445 Portuguese reach Cape Verde Islands (Atl. Oc.)
1448-1523 Wars between Denmark and Sweden rage
1450-1550 Some Popes are eager for war and indulge in nepotism and non-celibate excesses
1453 Sultan Mehmet II conquers Constantinople; brings an end to the Byzantine Empire

'Now Mohammed reigns over us!'
Pope Pius II

1453 Johan Gutenberg, German printer, prints books with movable-type, as the Chinese did before
1453 Nicolas Copernicus, Polish astronomer, develops his heliocentric view of the solar system; the earth rotates around the sun
1458 Aztec Empire extends through present Mexico and Guatemala
c 1460 Chinese Emperor Zhengtong blocks further maritime expansion by banning ships with more than one mast; *The Middle Empire* goes into isolation

1463 First meeting of the States General; representatives of the Burgundy States meet in Brussels
1467-1477 Reign of Charles (the Bold), Duke of Burgundy; obtains Lorraine, Upper-Alsace, Gelderland and hegemony over the Bishopric Principality of Liège

1469-1536 Life of Desiderius Erasmus, Dutch Renaissance humanist, Catholic priest and theologian; greatly influences humanism

1469 Infante Ferdinand of Aragon (Sp.) marries Infanta Isabella of Castile (Sp.); leads to a unified Spain in 1492

1473 Charles the Bold acquires the right to succeed to the Duchy of Gelderland

1475 Charles the Bold annexes Lorraine (Fr.) and joins Burgundy (Fr.) with Franche-Comté (Fr.)
1476 Charles the Bold fails to occupy the Swiss Confederacy which remains independent from then on

1477-1482 Reign of Mary (the Rich), Duchess of Burgundy
1477 'The Great Privilege' Mary the Rich signs a charter under which the provinces and the towns recover their rights

Habsburg Netherlands

1477 'Happy Arrival' Mary of Burgundy marries Maximilian I of Austria, Holy Roman Emperor; joins the Habsburg House with the Burgundy House, the Low Countries transferred into Habsburg's hands

1479 'Spanish Inquisition' Tribunal established by the monarchs Ferdinand and Isabella to maintain Catholic orthodoxy
1480 Russians refuse to pay tribute to the Golden Horde; end of Mongol yoke in eastern Europe
1481 First *auto-da-fé* (act of faith) at instigation of the Spanish Inquisition; heretics burnt at the stake

1482-1494 Maximilian I, Regent of the Low Countries

Low Countries

c 1485 Hieronymus Bosch, Dutch painter creates his magnum opus *The Garden of Earthly Desires*

1494-1506 Reign of Philip IV (the Handsome), Duke of Burgundy
1494-1533 Life of Lucas van Leyden, Dutch painter; progresses from Gothic to Renaissance style

1496 Philip the Handsome marries Joanna I of Castile (the Mad), who inherits Spain and the colonies in America; initiates the Habsburg dynasty in Spain

Wider World

1487 Bartholomeus Dias, Portuguese explorer, rounds Cape of Good Hope
1489 Venice takes control of Cyprus (Gr./Turk.)
1492 'Alhambra Decree' Monarchs Ferdinand and Isabella expel all Jews from Spain, unless they convert to Catholicism; Spain impoverished financially and scientifically
1492 Christopher Columbus, Italian explorer, reaches the Caribbean with the Santa Maria (length 30 metres)
1494 'Treaty of Tordesillas (Sp.)' Spanish and Portuguese monarchs divide, with consent of the Spanish-born Pope Alexander VI, newly discovered lands outside Europe between Spain and Portugal, along a meridian west of the Cape Verde Islands
1494 Luca Pacioli, Italian mathematician and Franciscan friar, introduces the double-entry accounting system; improves insight into trading results

1495-1521 Rule of Emmanuel I of Portugal; opens trading posts in Africa, Brazil, China, India, Indonesia and Japan

1497 Leonardo da Vinci, Italian 'uomo universale' (universal man), paints his masterpiece *The Last Supper*
1498 Vasco da Gama, Portuguese explorer, conquers Calcutta (India)

1499 Amerigo Vespucci, Italian navigator, explores the coast of Brazil for Portugal
1499 Giovanni Caboto, Venetian explorer, rediscovers Newfoundland (Can.)

1500 Charles V, born in Ghent (E. Fla.), as the eldest son of Philip the Handsome and Joanna the Mad

1503-1513 Alfonso de Albuquerque, Portuguese nobleman, establishes a colonial empire in Asia; acts as Viceroy of Portuguese India

1506 Charles V inherits the Low Countries and the Duchy of Burgundy
1506-1515 Margaret of Austria acts for Charles V as Regent of the Low Countries and Maximilian I acts as Regent for Charles V's other possessions

1508-1512 Buonarroti Michelangelo, Italian painter, starts painting the frescoes in the *Sistine Chapel* of the Vatican in Rome
1509-1564 Life of John Calvin, French theologian and reformer; founder of the Calvinist faith

From 1510 Antwerp develops into the financial centre of the world

1511 Alfonso de Albuquerque conquers Malacca (Malay Peninsula)

1512-1594 Life of Gerardus Mercator, Flemish cartographer

1513 Portuguese reach Japan

1515 Erasmus writes *Laus Stultitae* (The Praise of Folly)

'Where Folly appears, trouble disappears'
ERASMUS

1516 Sir Thomas More, English Renaissance humanist, describes an ideal political system in his novel *Utopia*
1516 Ottoman Turks conquer Palestine (Isr.) and Syria

1516 Niccolò Machiavelli, Italian diplomat and politician, writes *Il Principe* (The Prince)

'...a wise prince should establish himself on that which is in his own control and not in that of others; he must endeavour to avoid hatred, as is noted'
MACHIAVALLI

1516-1556 Reign of Charles V, King of Spain and the Spanish colonies

1517 Martin Luther, German monk, nails his 95 Theses to the door of the Wittenberg (Ger.) Church; beginning of the Protestant Reformation
1518 Tizian Vecelli, Italian painter completes his painting *Assumption of the Virgin*
1519-1521 Ferdinand Magellan, Portuguese explorer, makes the first circumnavigation of the earth, in the service of Charles V
1519-1534 Hernando Cortés and Francisco Pizarro, *Conquistadores* (Conquerors), put an end to the Aztec and Inca civilisations in Middle and South America

1519-1556 Charles V, Holy Roman Emperor and King of Spain

'The Empire on which the sun never sets'
POPULAR SAYING DURING SPAIN'S GOLDEN AGE

1520-1566 Suleiman I (the Magnificent), Sultan of the Ottoman Empire; enlarges his realm into the Balkans, whilst overseeing artistic, literary and architectural developments

1520 Martin Luther's books appear in Antwerp; his doctrine spreads widely

1521 'Diet of Worms (Ger.)' Assembly of the Estates of the Holy Roman Empire condemns the doctrine of Martin Luther
1521 Suleiman the Magnificent occupies Belgrade (Serb.)

1532 Martin Afonso de Souza, Portuguese nobleman, begins the colonisation of Brazil
1522-1523 Reign of Pope Adrian VI, the only pope from the Low Countries

1522 Start of the Counter Reformation in the Low Countries; introduction of baroque style to make churches more attractive
1523 Charles V annexes Drenthe, Friesland, Gelderland and Groningen
1523 Two Augustinian friars are the first Protestant martyrs to be burnt at the stake in Brussels

1523 Gustav I, King of Sweden, proclaims full independence from Denmark; marking the end of the Kalmar Union
1524-1580 Life of Luis Vaz de Camões, Portugal's greatest poet; his epic work *The Lusiads* focuses on the Portuguese voyages of discovery

1525 Priests of Woerden (S. Hol.) burned at the stake
1525-1569 Life of Pieter Bruegel the Elder, Flemish painter; father of Pieter Brueghel the Younger and Jan Brueghel the Elder, who are also Flemish painters

1526 Ottoman Turks, under Suleiman the Magnificent, defeat the Hungarian Army; King Louis II of Hungary dies
1526 Zahir Mohammed Babar, Muslim from Turkey, founds the Mughal Empire in India; fosters Persian artistic and literary influence in India
1527 Charles V's soldiers plunder Rome

1528 Charles V secularises Utrecht; Bishop retains ecclesiastical powers

1529 Ottoman Turks attack Vienna (Austria) in vain
1530 Charles V gives Malta to the Knights of St John
1530-1555 Wars among the Lutheran and Catholic monarchs of Germany

Low Countries

1531 Charles V declares the Low Countries to be a unified entity; State Council established in Brussels

1533-1584 Life of William I (the Silent), Prince of Orange; Father of the Fatherland

1544 William of Nassau inherits the Principality of Orange (Fr.) from his cousin René of Chalôn, Stadtholder of Gelderland, Holland, Utrecht and Zeeland

1547-1619 Life of Johan van Oldenbarnevelt, Grand Pensionary of Holland and statesman

Wider World

1534 'Act of Supremacy' grants ecclesiastical authority to the monarchy; permits Henry VIII, King of England, to divorce his first wife

c 1534 Spaniards wipe out the Inca Empire

1534 Ignatius Loyola, Spanish priest, founds the Society of Jesus (Jesuits); combats the Reformation

1535 Jacques Cartier, French explorer, discovers the St Lawrence River (Can.)

1536 John of Leyden, Dutch clergyman, Anabaptist leader in Munster (Ger.); tortured to death for his faith

1536 Calvin preaches his faith in Geneva (Switz.)

1539-1604 Life of Faustus Socinus, Italian theologian, advocates a rational interpretation of the Bible

1543 Suleiman the Magnificent and François I of France occupy Nice (Fr.); pinnacle in the Franco-Ottoman Alliance

1547-1584 Reign of Tsar Ivan IV (the Terrible), transforms Russia into a multi-ethnic and multiconfessional state; limits the freedom of the peasants to serfdom

'Je maintiendrai'

'I shall maintain', MOTTO OF ORANGE

1548 'Transaction of Augsburg (Ger.)' Seventeen Netherlands Provinces become a political and independent part of the Burgundy Circle (Kreitz) of the Holy Roman Empire

1548 Silver mines discovered in Mexico and Peru

1548 'Pragmatic Sanction' Sovereignty of the Seventeen Netherlands Provinces passes to the Emperor's heirs in perpetuity
1548-1620 Life of Simon Stevin, Flemish mathematician and engineer, learns about decimal fractions; lays mathematical basis for the construction of fortifications
1550-1650 Amsterdam develops into the financial centre of the world
1550-1850 *Little Ice Age* brings colder winters to Europe; rivers in the Low Countries often deeply freeze over

1555 Ivan the Terrible, conquers the Tatars and gets control of Astrakhan (Rus.)
1555 'Diet of Augsburg' Roman Catholic Princes of Germany acknowledge the principle which gives each Prince the power to decide the religion of their subjects
1555 Charles V abdicates; the Habsburg Empire breaks up into Austrian and Spanish branches

Spanish Netherlands

1555 Charles V's son Philip II inherits Spain, its American colonies, the Low Countries and the Italian territories

1555 Charles V's brother Ferdinand I, Archduke of Austria, remains in possession of the dynastic Habsburg lands in Austria and Germany

1555-1598 Reign of Philip II, King of Spain

1555-1700 Calvinists, Germans, Huguenots and Jews from Flanders and Wallonia migrate into the northern Low Countries; which helps to forge trade and prosperity

1556 Ferdinand I succeeds as Holy Roman Emperor

1556-1605 Akbar (the Great) rules the Mughal Empire in India; exercises tolerance towards other religions

1557 Portuguese settle in the Macau peninsula (China) and keep it for nearly 450 years

1558-1603 Reign of Queen Elizabeth I (the Virgin Queen) of England and Ireland; last monarch of the Tudor dynasty

1559 Philip II departs from Brussels to Spain; eight consecutive Regents succeed him

'Non los Estados, ma vos, vos, vos!'

'*Not the States, but thou, thou, thou*!' PHILIP II BLAMES WILLIAM OF ORANGE AT HIS DEPARTURE

1559-1567 Margaret of Parma, Regent of the Spanish Netherlands

1562-1576 Maximilian II of Austria, Holy Roman Emperor; Protestantism reaches its pinnacle

1562-1598 'Wars of Religion' between Huguenots and Roman Catholics in France

1563-1570 'Northern Seven Years' War' between Denmark and Sweden; Sweden gains its independence

1564 William of Orange addressing the State Council about the freedom of religion

'I cannot approve that monarchs desire to rule over the conscience of their subjects and deprive them of faith and religion'

WILLIAM OF ORANGE

1565 Sir Walter Raleigh, English writer and explorer, introduces tobacco and potatoes to Europe from America

1566 'Petition of Compromise' Two hundred noblemen request denunciation of the Inquisition and return of ancient privileges

'Ce ne sont que les Gueux'

'*They are only Beggars*', WHISPERS A COUNSELLOR TO MARGARET OF PARMA, AFTER WHICH THE SOBRIQUET *Gueux* TURNS INTO A NAME OF HONOUR

1566 'Iconoclasm' Fury by the Protestants sweeps from Steenvoorde (Fr.) across the Roman Catholic churches in the Low Countries; beginning of the revolt against Philip II

1567-1574 Reign of Regent Duke of Alba, whose 'Council of Troubles' orders beheading of Counts Van Egmond and Van Horne and levies a Tenth Penny sales tax

1567-1625 Life of Count Maurice of Nassau

1568-1648 'The Eighty Years' War' rages between Spain and the Low Countries

1568 'Battle of Heiligerlee (Gro.)' Counts Adolf and Louis of Nassau defeat the Spaniards; first victory in the Eighty Years' War

1568-1588 Reign of Shogun Ashikaga Yoshiaki; restores effective central authority in the capital of Kyoto, beginning of Japanese unity

1569-1573 *Biblia Regia* Synoptic publication of the Bible in five languages by Christofel Patijn, French printer in Antwerp

1569-1795' Union of Lublin' Sigismund II of Poland unites the Kingdom of Poland and the Grand Duchy of Lithuania into a single state, the Polish-Lithuanian Commonwealth; becomes one of the largest and most densely populated countries of Europe

1570 Andrea Palladio, Italian Renaissance architect, writes *The Four Books of Architecture*

1571 Venice is forced to hand over Cyprus to Ottoman Turks

1571 Spain takes possession of the Philippines; Manila develops into the trade centre for silver between Asia, Europe and Mexico

1571 Moscow plundered by the Crimean-Tatar Army

1571 'Battle of Lepanto (Gr.)' Italian and Spanish fleets under Don John of Austria, the illegitimate son of Charles V, defeat the Turkish fleet; eliminates the Turkish threat to Europe by sea

1572 Sea-Beggars (maritime force established by the Protestant rebels) under Count Lumey, nobleman from Liège, seize the port of Brielle (S. Hol.); citizens seize many other towns

1572 First free assembly of the States of Holland in Dordrecht (S. Hol.); appoints William of Orange Stadtholder of Holland

1572 'St Bartholomew's Day' Massacre of Huguenots by Roman Catholics in France; brings about the 'Fourth War of Religion' in France

1572-1573 'Siege of Haarlem (N. Hol.)' Kenau Simonsdochter Hasselaer, a female citizen, acts courageously

1572-1589 Henry IV de Bourbon, King of Navarra; leader of the Huguenots in France

1572-1632 Ten thousands of men, from Brabant, Flanders and Walloon provinces, settle in liberated towns in Holland and Zeeland which owe their economic and cultural growth to this influx

1573 'Alkmaar's (N. Hol.) Relief' Spanish troops end the siege after the Dutch pierced the dykes

'Victory starts from Alkmaar!'
SLOGAN IN THE LOW COUNTRIES

1574 Spanish Army defeat the States Army near Mook (N. Lim.); counts Louis and Henry of Nassau killed
1574 Philips II replaces Alba as Regent of the Spanish Netherlands by Luis de Requesens, Spanish diplomat
1574 'Leyden's (S. Hol.) Relief' Sea Beggars break the Spanish Army's siege
1575 University of Leyden founded at the initiative of William of Orange
1576 'Spanish Fury' Mutinous Spanish soldiers sack Antwerp
1576 'Pacification of Ghent (E. Flan.)' Agreement among the Seventeen Provinces to unite; William of Orange asserts his leadership
1576 States General of The Netherlands organised as governing body

1576-1612 Rudolf II of Austria, King of Hungary, Croatia and Bohemia, Holy Roman Emperor, reinforces the difference between Protestants and Roman Catholics; leads to the 'Thirty Years' War'

1576-1578 Philip II appoints Don Juan of Austria as Regent
1577 'Eternal Edict' Don Juan signs armistice with the States General; but breaks the truce by taking Namur the same year
1577 Adrian Coenen, fishmonger and auctioneer in Scheveningen (S. Hol.) writes and sketches *The Visboeck*; oldest record of the creatures of the North Sea

1577 Accademia di San Luca, first art academy, founded in Rome

1577-1581 Reign of Matthias, Archduke of Austria, installed by the States General as Regent General as a replacement for Don Juan

1577-1640 Life of Peter Paul Rubens, painter from Antwerp
1577-1660 Life of Jacob Cats, Pensionary of Holland and poet; constructs his residence *Catshuis* in The Hague

'Children are a hindrance'
'FATHER' CATS, FORGETTING HE WAS ONCE A CHILD TOO

1578 Mongol leader Altan Khan of China bestows title of Dalai Lama (Ocean of Wisdom) on Sonam Gyatso, leader of Tibetan Buddhism

1578-1592 Regent Alessandro Farnese, Duke of Parma and grandson of Charles V, wins the Walloon Provinces for Spain and the Roman Catholic faith
1579 The Seventeen Provinces are separated by the struggle between Farnese of Parma and William of Orange
1579 'Union of Arras (Fr.)' Roman Catholic provinces Artois, Hainault and Walloon-Flanders unite and submit to Philip II and the Roman Catholic Church; northern provinces of Groningen and Overijssel join later
1579 'Union of Utrecht' Seven Calvinist northern provinces and the cities of Antwerp, Bruges, Brussels, Ghent, Ypres and Mechlin in the southern Netherlands unite and continue the struggle against Philip II

1580 Alba conquers Portugal for the Spanish monarch

1580 Philip II puts a bounty on the head of William of Orange

1580-1640 Dynastic union between the monarchies of Portugal and Spain; Philip II of Spain was crowned Philip I of Portugal in 1581

1581 'Act of Abjuration' Philip II formally repudiated by the States of Brabant, Friesland, Gelderland, Holland, Utrecht, Flanders and Zeeland; Act serves as inspiration for the Declaration of Independence of the United States of America in 1782

1581-1588 Regent Farnese conquers the provinces Brabant, Flanders, Limburg and Gelderland

1584 Sir Walter Raleigh founds settlements in Virginia (US)

1584 William of Orange murdered in Delft (S. Hol.); Prince Maurice of Nassau, 16 years old, assumes his duties

'Mon Dieu, ayez pitié de moi et de votre pauvre peuple'
'My God, have pity on me and your poor people', LAST WORDS OF WILLIAM OF ORANGE

1585 Regent Farnese conquers Antwerp, defended by Marnix of St Aldegonde, Flemish writer and statesman; Scheldt river blocked for two centuries, damages Antwerp's position as a trade city

1585 Massive emigration from Brabant and Flanders to the north; knowledge and capital bring prosperity

1585 Robert Dudley, Earl of Leicester and favourite of Elizabeth I of England, sent to give support to the northern Netherlands

1585-1625 Prince Maurice of Nassau, Stadtholder of Holland and Zeeland

1587 Roman Catholic Mary, Queen of Scots, beheaded after she is implicated in a plot to murder her cousin, Protestant Queen Elizabeth I of England

1588 Spanish Armada defeated near Dunkirk (Fr.) by English fleet under Admiral Lord Howard and Sir Francis Drake, English privateer and navigator; invasion of England averted

'I know I have the body of a weak and feeble woman; but I have the heart and stomach of a King, and of a King of England too'
QUEEN ELIZABETH I TO HER TROOPS

1588-1648 Reign of Christian IV, King of Denmark-Norway for 59 years; initiates many reforms and projects

United Provinces / Spanish Netherlands

1588-1795 Republic of the Seven United Provinces ofThe Netherlands; confederation of sovereign provinces forms the first modern democracy since the former Greek democracy
1589 Regent Farnese recalled; separation of the Low Countries completed

1589-1610 Reign of King Henry IV of France, after conversion to the Roman Catholic faith

'Paris vaut bien une messe'
'Paris is worth a mass', HENRY IV

1590 'Peat-boat of Breda' City of Breda (N. Bra.) recaptured by means of a trick by the United Provinces' Army

1591 William Shakespeare, English playwright and poet, writes his famous play *Romeo and Juliet*

1592 Jan Huygen van Linschoten, Dutch explorer, returns from the East and publishes *Itinerario,* containing the secret Portuguese sea route to India

1592 Spain sells its rights to the Spice Islands (Maluku, Indon.) to Portugal
1592-1598 Japan invades Korea

1594 'Long-Distance Company' founded by Amsterdam's merchants, breaks the pepper monopoly of the Portuguese
1595-1597 First voyage by the Dutch to East Asia; captain Cornelis Houtman lands at Bantam, Java (Indon.)

1596 Johan of Oldenbarnevelt concludes a treaty with England and France against Spain; first international recognition of the United Provinces

1596-1597 'The Saved House' William Barentsz, Dutch captain, spends the winter at Nova Zembla (N. Ice Sea)

1596-1650 Life of René Descartes, French philosopher and mathematician, spends most of his adult life in the Low Countries; lays the basis of rationalism

'Cogito ergo sum'
'*I think, therefore I am*', DESCARTES

1596-1687 Life of Constantijn Huygens, Dutch poet, diplomat and composer

1598 'Edict of Nantes' issued by Henry IV, grants French Protestants equal rights with Roman Catholics

1598 Wybrant Warwijck, Dutch captain, discovers the uninhabited island of Mauritius (Ind. Oc.)

1598-1621 Joint rule by Archduke Albert of Austria and his wife Infanta Isabella of Spain over the Spanish Netherlands; United Provinces deny their sovereignty

1598-1621 Philip III leaves the government of Spain in the hands of his confidant the Duke of Lerma

1600 'East India Company (EIC)' First Joint-Stock Company, formed in London, to pursue trade with East Indies

'Passion for pepper seemed to burn like a flame of love in the breast of Dutch and English adventurers'
JOSEPH CONRAD IN *Lord Jim*

1600 Maurice of Nassau invades Flanders to liberate Ostend (W. Flan.), last remaining Protestant stronghold in the Roman Catholic Spanish Netherlands

1600 'Battle of Newport (W. Flan.)' Maurice of Nassau defeats the Spaniards; but retreats to the United Provinces

From 1600 Ireland remains devastated and poor after long years of revolts against England

1600-1700 Germans, Huguenots, Spanish and Portuguese Jews, find shelter in the United Provinces; where they strengthen the economy

1600-1917 Eleven wars rage between Russia and the Ottoman Empire; Russia enlarges its territory
1601 Michaelangelo Caravaggio, Italian painter, makes his famous painting *Crucifixion of St Peter*
1601 Shakespeare writes another famous play *Hamlet, Prince of Denmark*

'To be, or not to be, that is the question'
SHAKESPEARE

1601-1604 'Siege of Ostend' Ambroglio, Spanish general, leads the siege until the destruction of the city is complete
1602 'Verenigde Oost-Indische Compagnie (VOC) (United East Indies Company)' Joint-Stock Company established to pursue trade with the East; beginning of Dutch colonial expansion
1602 United Provinces establish a garrison in Emden on the river Elbe (Ger.)

1603-1625 'Union of the Crowns' King James VI of Scotland also reigns as King James I of England and Ireland; rules the three kingdoms for twenty-two years, with the title of King of Great Britain
1605 Miguel de Cervantes, Spanish novelist, completes the romance of chivalry *Don Quixote*

1605 'Gunpowder Plot' Failed assassination attempt on King James I by a group of English Roman Catholics led by Guy Fawkes

1606 Dutch captain Willem Janszoon sights Australia with the merchant-ship 'Dyfken'

1607 Jamestown founded in Virginia (US); becomes first English colony in North America

1608 French found the colony of Québec (Can.)

1609 French establish a trading foothold in present Louisiana (US)

1609 Count of Lerma deports 150,000 Moriscos (Spaniards, who adhere to Islamic faith) to North Africa; this ethnic cleansing impoverishes Spain financially and intellectually

1609 Hugo Grotius, Dutch jurist, philosopher and poet, writes *Mare Liberum* (The Free Sea); his contribution to international law advocates free trade and free access to sea

1609-1619 Theological controversy between Remonstrants under Jacobus Arminius, professor of theology at Leyden and Calvinists under theologian Franciscus Gomarus at Amsterdam

1609-1621 'Twelve Years' Truce' Philip III acknowledges the United Provinces a Free State for the duration of the truce; river Scheldt remains closed

1609 Henry Hudson, English navigator, explores under the auspices of the VOC the island of Manhatten, which is now New York; lays the foundation for Dutch colonisation of the region

c 1610 Simon the Dancer, Dutch privateer, operates in northern African waters with a 'Letter of Marque and Reprisal' issued by the VOC

1611 Hendrik Brouwer, Dutch explorer, sails via the Roaring Forties, between the latitudes of 40 and 49 degree, to Java, Netherlands East Indies; cuts the one year journey by half

1611-1632 Reign of Gustav II Adolf, King of Sweden; sees his country grow into the third largest state in Europe

1612 Jan Adriaenszoon Leeghwater, Dutch windmill builder, reclaims the Beemster (N. Hol.) polder

1612-1619 Reign of Matthias of Austria, Holy Roman Emperor
1613–1645 Reign of Michael I of Russia, first Tsar of the House of Romanov

1618 Philip William of Orange, eldest son of William of Orange dies; Maurice of Nassau inherits the title of Prince of Orange

1618 'Defenestration of Prague (Czech.)' Protestant noblemen throw Roman Catholic representatives of Ferdinand II of Germany out of a window; which exacerbates the Bohemian Revolt and precipitates the Thirty Years' War

1618-1619 *Synod of Dordrecht* (S. Hol.) Assembly of the Dutch Reformed Church to settle the controversy caused by the rise of Remonstrants; initiates the official Dutch Bible translation

1618-1648 'Thirty Years' War' polarises Europe on religious grounds; destructive conflict fought primarily, though not exclusively in Germany, takes 8 million lives and fundamentally changes the political map of Europe

1619 Treaty between EIC and VOC mediated by Hugo Grotius; spice trade is divided between the two companies
1619 Jan Pietersz Coen, Dutch Regent General of the VOC, conquers Jayakarta; renames it Batavia as capital of Netherlands East Indies (now Jakarta)

'And do not despair'
MOTTO OF COEN

1619 First slaves from Africa arrive in Virginia (US)

1619 Johan van Oldenbarnevelt accused of high treason by Prince Maurice and is beheaded

'Men, do not believe that I am a traitor, I have acted rightly and faithfully as a brave patriot and so I will die'
JOHAN VAN OLDENBARNEVELT AT THE SCAFFOLD TO THE PEOPLE, AND TO THE EXECUTIONER:
'Make it short'

1619-1620 Frederick V (the Winter King), King of Bohemia, leader of the Protestants during the Thirty Years' War, is defeated in the 'Battle of the White Mountain (Prague, Czech.)' by the German Imperial Army; remains in exile in The Hague for the remainder of his life
1619-1637 Reign of Ferdinand II of Austria, Holy Roman Emperor; his ultra-Roman Catholic intolerance impedes the peace process during the Thirty Years' War

1620 Cornelis Drebbel, Dutch inventor, navigates the river Thames (Eng.) with the first submarine
1620 Pilgrim Fathers sail to Massachusetts (US) with the Mayflower after a 12 year stay in Leyden (S. Hol.); found the Plymouth colony
1621 Hugo Grotius, jailed for his Remonstrant beliefs, escapes from Castle Loevestein (S. Hol.) in a book chest; flees to Paris
1621 VOC Army under Jan Pieterszoon Coen, massacres the population of the Banda Islands (Maluku, Netherlands East Indies)

1621-1625 Flemish painter Peter Paul Rubens, completes 24 paintings about the life of the Italian Maria de Medici

1621-1633 Infanta Isabella of Spain, Regent over the Spanish Netherlands, after the death of her husband Duke Albert of Austria

1621-1665 Philip IV, King of Spain, leaves the government in the hands of Count Olivares; war with the United Provinces rages on for 27 years, during which the decline of the Spanish economy continues

1621-1730 West Indies Company (WIC); obtains Dutch monopoly of the slave trade

1622-1891 Indians have to endure more than 250 years of wars in northern America with western immigrants

1623-1662 Life of Blaise Pascal, French mathematician and philosopher, his magnum opus is *Pensées*

1

1 2 1

1 3 3 1

1 4 6 4 1

Pascal's Triangle

1624 Frans Hals, painter from Antwerp, creates his masterpiece *The Laughing Cavalier* in Haarlem (N. Hol.)

1624 Nieuw Amsterdam, now New York, founded by WIC, with Flemish and Walloon immigrants

1624-1625 'Siege of Breda (N. Bra.)' Abrogio Spinola, Spanish general, conquers the famished city; turns out to be a Pyrrhic victory

1624-1661 VOC maintains fortress Zeelandia, a trading post on the island of Taiwan (Ind. Oc.)

1625-1629 Christian IV, King of Denmark and Duke of Schleswig-Holstein (Ger.), unsuccessfully leads the Protestants during the Thirty Years' War against the Holy Roman Emperor

1625-1647 Reign of Frederick Henry (Conqueror of Towns), Prince of Orange, Count of Nassau and Stadtholder of Gelderland, Holland, Overijssel, Utrecht and Zeeland

1625 Hugo Grotius lays the basis for international law with his work *De iure belli ac pacis* (on the Law of War and Peace)

'Fully convinced that there is a common law among nations, which is valid alike for war and in war'
HUGO GROTIUS

1628 Piet Hein, Dutch Admiral, captures a Spanish treasure fleet; the loot finances the United Provinces Army

1628 Huguenots surrender to Cardinal de Richelieu, influential French statesman, in La Rochelle (Fr.)

1628 William Harvey, English physician, is the first to correctly describe the properties of blood

1629 Prince Frederick Henry captures 's-Hertogenbosch (N. Bra.); turning point in the war with Spain

1630 WIC conquers Pernambuco (Braz.)

1630-1632 Gustav II Adolf, King of Sweden, leads the Protestants during the Thirty Years' War and adds swaths of German land to his realm; international recognition of Sweden's stature

1632 Flemish painter Sir Anthony van Dyck, becomes the leading court painter in England

1632-1677 Life of Baruch de Spinoza, Dutch philosopher and lens grinder of Portuguese/Jewish origin, writes his magnum opus *The Ethics*

'The Torah betrays the human spirit so much, that it cannot possibly be written or inspired by God'

CONCLUDES SPINOZA, AFTER WHICH HE IS EXCOMMUNICATED

1632-1653 Shah Jahan I of the Mughal Empire, constructs the *Taj Mahal,* mausoleum in Agra (Ind.)

1632-1723 Life of Antonie van Leeuwenhoek, Dutch trader and scientist; improves the microscope and develops microbiology

1633 Galileo Galilei, Italian astronomer and philosopher, confirms Copernicus' heliocentric vision of the solar system; condemned by the Pope to lifelong house arrest

'Eppur si muove...'

'Nevertheless, it moves...',

WHISPERS GALILEI, SUBMITTING TO HIS HOUSE ARREST

1634-1641 Reign of Cardinal-Infante Ferdinand, Archduke of Austria, Regent of the Spanish Netherlands

1635 *L'Académie Française* Pre-eminent French learned body on matters pertaining to French language founded

1635 Armies of France and the United Provinces attack the Spanish Netherlands; French Army loots Tienen (Fl. Bra.)

1635-1640 Treaty between France, Sweden and the United Provinces against Spain and Austria

1635-1659 'Franco-Spanish War' Military conflict begins with French intervention in the Thirty Years' War

1636 Harvard University in Cambridge, Mass. (US) founded

1636-1637 *Tulipmania* Financial crisis occurs in the United Provinces as a result of speculation in the tulip trade

1637 Breda (N. Bra.) re-taken from the Spaniards; stimulates peace negotiations

1637-1863 Slave trade and forced labour in southern and northern America

1640-1688 Frederick William, Elector of Brandenburg and Duke of Prussia; setting Prussia up for elevation to kingdom

1641-1644 Francisco de Melo, Spanish nobleman, Regent of the Spanish Netherlands

1642 Montreal (Can.) founded by the French

1642 Rembrandt van Rijn, Dutch painter, completes his masterpiece *The Night Watch*

1642-1649 'Civil War' Oliver Cromwell, English military and political leader, defeats the royalists under Charles I, King of England

1642-1659 Abel Tasman, Dutch explorer, in the service of the VOC, discovers Tasmania (Aus.) and New Zealand

1643-1715 Reign of Louis XIV (the Sun King), King of France, at the pinnacle of absolutism

'L'état, c'est moi'
'I am the State', Louis XIV

1644-1647 Manuel de Castel Rodrigo, Portuguese nobleman, Regent of the Spanish Netherlands

1644-1911 Manchu Qing, the last imperial dynasty, rules China; expands into China proper and surrounding territories, Manchu dynasty integrates with Chinese culture

1645 French occupy Bethune (Fr.), Graveling (Zee.) and Kassel (Ger.); United Provinces take Hulst (Zee.) and occupy northern Flanders

1646 Capitulation of Tournai (Hain.) and Dunkirk (Fr.) to the French

1647-1650 William II of Orange, Stadtholder of Gelderland, Groningen, Holland, Overijssel, Utrecht and Zeeland

Low Countries	Wider World

1647-1656 Leopold William of Austria, Regent of Spanish Netherlands; reconquers French held Armentiéres, Komen, Lens and Landrecies (Fr.)

1648 George Fox, English dissenter, founds the religious *Society of Friends* (Quakers); proposing an uncompromising approach to the Christian faith

1648 'Peace of Westphalia (Ger.)' ends the Thirty Years' War; religious tolerance recognised, Holy Roman Empire fragmented into almost independent states

1648 'Peace of Munster (Ger.)' ends the Eighty Years' War; United Provinces obtain North Brabant, Maastricht (N. Lim.), Overmaasse (N. Lim.) and northern Flanders (Zee.), river Scheldt remains closed

1648-1665 Jacob van Campen, Dutch artist and architect, designs the *Amsterdam City Hall*; at that time the largest non-religious building in the world

1649 Dutch defeat the Spaniards at Ternate (Maluku, Netherlands East Indies); last battle of the Eighty Years' War, one year after the Peace of Munster

1649 Tsar Alexis I enslaves Russian peasants, now called serfs

1649 Charles I of England beheaded; Oliver Cromwell heads the Commonwealth of England, republican form of government replaces the monarchy

Age of Enlightenment

1650 Stadtholder William II dies; William III, born seven days later, becomes Prince of Orange

1650 Oliver Cromwell conquers Ireland

1650-1672 'First Period without Stadtholder' States of Gelderland, Holland, Overijssel, Utrecht and Zeeland appoint no Stadtholder; the United Provinces become a true Republic
1650-1702 Life of William III, Prince of Orange

1651 'Navigation Act' restricts use of foreign shipping for trade between England and its colonies; leads to three wars with the United Provinces

1652 Jan van Riebeeck, Dutch sailor, establishes a re-supply camp at Cape of Good Hope (S. Afr.) for the VOC; Boers (Dutch-African word for emigrant farmers from western Europe) increase their influence

1652 Oliver Cromwell conquers Scotland

1652 'Battle of Dungeness (Kent, Eng.)' Maarten Harpertszoon Tromp, Dutch Admiral, attaches a broom to the mast after his victory over the English fleet

'A naval hero, whose equal the earth has not often known and will not lightly find in the future'

JOHAN DE WITT'S FUNERAL ORATION FOR TROMP, 1653

1652-1654 'First Anglo-Dutch War'
1653 Johan de Witt, Dutch statesman, appointed Grand Pensionary of Holland

1653 Oliver Cromwell becomes Lord Protector of England, Scotland and Ireland

1654 'Treaty of Westminster' ends the First Anglo-Dutch War; contains a secret 'Act of Seclusion', excluding William III from being appointed to the Stadtholderate

1656 Diego Velázquez, Spanish painter, completes *Las Meninas* (Maids of Honour)

1656-1659 Juan José II of Austria, Regent of the Spanish Netherlands

1657 Christiaan Huygens, Dutch astronomer and mathematician, inventor of the pendulum clock; provides the basis for the probability theory

1657 France and England form an alliance against Spain, initiated by Oliver Cromwell; England receives Dunkirk (Fr.)

1658 'Battle of the Sound (Den.)' Jacob van Wassenaer Obdam, Dutch Admiral, defeats the fleet of King Charles X Gustav of Sweden, supported by a nearby anchored English fleet; maintains free passage to the Baltic Sea

'Voilà votre religion'

'That is your religion', says Charles X, producing a golden coin, in a discussion with a Dutch diplomat

1658 VOC conquers Ceylon (Sri Lanka), previously Portuguese territory; secures cinnamon trade for the Dutch

1658 Turenne, Marshal of France, defeats the Spanish Army near Dunkirk (Fr.)

1659 Joost van den Vondel, Dutch poet and playwright, best known for his play *Gijsbrecht van Amstel*

'Farewell my Amstelland; expect another Lord'

Final phrase of the Gijsbrecht

1659 'Treaty of Pyrenees' ends the Franco-Spanish War; France acquires Artois (Fr.), Roussillon (Fr.) and northern Catalonia (Sp.)

1660 'Restoration' Monarchy of England, Scotland and Ireland restored under King Charles II; House of Stuart reigns again

1661-1722 Reign of Manchu Qing Emperor Kangxi; biggest expansion of China with addition of Mongolia, Chinese dictionary compiled

1662 Joan Blaeu, Dutch cartographer and publisher, prints *Atlas Major* with 600 maps ocovering the entire world

1664 Ottoman Turks conquer Hungary

1665-1667 'Second Anglo-Dutch War' England tries in vain to end Dutch domination of world trade

1666 Great Fire of London

1666 Johannes Vermeer, Dutch painter, famous for his *Girl with a Pearl Earring*
1667 'Raid on the Medway (Eng.)' Michiel de Ruyter (Good Father), Dutch Admiral, under command of Cornelis de Witt, Deputy of the States of Holland, sails up the river Medway as far as Chatham and destroys the British fleet
1667 'Treaty of Breda (N. Bra.)' ends the Second Anglo-Dutch War; New Amsterdam exchanged for Surinam (Netherlands West Indies) to trade slaves

1667 John Milton, English poet, publishes his best known epic poem *Paradise Lost*

1667-1668 'War of Devolution' Spain and France fight over the Spanish Netherlands
1668 'Triple Alliance of 1668' England, Sweden and the United Provinces form a coalition to halt the expansion of France

1668 'Treaty of Aix-la-Chappelle (Ger.)' ends War of Devolution; France gains French-Flanders and the coastal swath up to Newport (W. Flan.) from Spain and returns Franche-Comté (Fr.)
1668 Independence of Portugal recognised by Spain

1671 United Provinces conclude an alliance with Spain to defend themselves against imperialistic France

1672 Charles II engages William van der Velde the Elder and his son William the Younger, both Dutch maritime painters

1672 Brothers Johan and Cornelis de Witt slaughtered by a mob in The Hague

'Tear me into pieces; you don't get out, what is not inside'
CORNELIS DE WITT, UNDER TORTURE

1672-1674 'Third Anglo-Dutch War' Michiel de Ruyter's triple victories over the Anglo-French fleets ward off invasion
1672-1678 'Franco-Dutch War' France, Sweden and England, later joined by the Holy Roman Empire and Spain form a quadruple alliance against the United Provinces; French Army penetrates into the United Provinces

'The country was defenceless, the governors desperate and the people distraught'
1672, YEAR OF DISASTER

1672-1702 William III Stadtholder of Gelderland, Holland, Overijssel, Utrecht and Zeeland

1673 England withdraws from the Franco-Dutch War; Spain, United Provinces, Holy Roman Empire and Brandenburg form an alliance against France

1673 The United Provinces are now one of the powerful states of Europe; lead the alliance against Louis XIV of France

1674 Poles elect Jan Sobieski as their king

1676 Michiel de Ruyter perishes after a battle near Messina (It.)

1677 Jean Racine, French playwright, publishes *Phèdre*

1677 Spinoza publishes *Ethics*

'Everything which is perfect, is equally difficult and rare'
FINAL PHRASE OF ETHICS

1678 'Peace of Nijmegen (Gel.)' ends the Franco-Dutch war; France receives Bouillon, Condé, Cambrai and Maubeuge (Fr.), United Provinces receive Maastricht (N. Lim.)

1682 VOC expels the last English people from the island of Java (Netherlands East Indies)

1682-1725 Reign of Tsar Peter I (the Great) of Russia; carries out policy of modernisation and expansion, which makes Russia a major European power
1683 'Battle of Vienna' Ottoman siege of Vienna broken by Polish King Jan III and support of Pope Innocent XI; turning point in Ottoman Empire's advance into Europe
1684 British EIC receives permission to build a trading station in Canton (Chin.)

'There is concern that in the coming centuries China will collide with the countries from the West'
EMPEROR K'ANG HSI

1685 Louis XIV revokes Edict of Nantes; Huguenots flee from France and settle in the United Provinces and Germany
1687 Sir Isaac Newton, English philosopher and physicist, develops his ideas in *Philosophiae Naturalis Principia Mathematica*; leads to a scientific revolution
1688 "Glorious Revolution' Members of the English nobility invite Stadtholder William III and Princess Mary to defend the liberties of England and to depose King James II; William III invades England and defeats his father-in-law James II, who flees to France

1688-1697 'Nine Years' War' pits King Louis XIV against a Grand Alliance of Stadtholder-King William III, Holy Roman Emperor Leopold I, King Charles II of Spain and Duke Victor Amadeus II of Savoy

1689 'Treaty of Nerchinsk (Siberia)' China's first treaty with a European power, Russia, drafted in Latin; the river Amur forms the border between the countries

1689-1702 King-Stadtholder William III and Queen Mary II govern England as joint sovereigns; parliament predominates
1690 John Locke, English philosopher and physician, publishes *Essay concerning Human Understanding*; Father of Liberalism
1690 'Battle of the Boyne (Irl.)' William III defeats James II; turning point in the defence of the crown

'There is but one manner to see your country never losing and that is to die in the last ditch'
WILLIAM III

1692 Edward Lloyd from Wales (UK) opens Lloyd's Coffee House where insurance deals are concluded; blossoming of insurance market
1692 Christians officially tolerated in China
1693 Colbertism introduced in France; promotes industry over agriculture

1696 John William Friso of Nassau-Dietz appointed Stadtholder in Friesland and Groningen; his mother acts as Regent
1697 Tsar Peter the Great visits the United Provinces and England to study shipbuilding
1697 'Treaty of Ryswyck (S. Hol.)' Settles the Nine Years' War; France surrenders Freiburg (Ger.) to the Holy Roman Empire and regains Saint-Dominique (Haiti) and Nova Scotia (Can.), Spain recovers Catalonia (Sp.), Mons (Hain.), Luxembourg and Kortrijk (W. Flan.), Duchy of Lorraine (Fr.) restored, United Provinces garrison the chief barrier fortresses in the Spanish Netherlands, including Namur and Ypres (W. Flan.)

1698 *Goose Step* introduced by Prussian Army
1699 French develop the colony of Louisiana (US)

1702 With the death of the childless William III, John William Friso of Nassau-Dietz inherits the title of Prince of Orange from his distant cousin

1702-1747 'Second Period without Stadtholder' In the provinces Gelderland, Holland, Overijssel, Utrecht and Zeeland no Stadtholder appointed

1707 John William Friso of Orange-Nassau comes of age; exercises the function of Stadtholder of Friesland and Groningen

From 1700 Industrial Revolution in England; boosted by cheap coal and high wages

1700-1721 'Great Northern War' Conflict in which a coalition led by Peter I of Russia, Frederick IV of Denmark-Norway and Augustus II of Saxon-Poland-Lithuania successfully contests Swedish supremacy in Central and East Europe

1701-1714 'War of Spanish Succession' Retaliation against Louis XIV's acceptance of the Spanish crown for his grandson Philip V, first Bourbon King of Spain; Leopold I, Holy Roman Emperor, forms an alliance with Denmark, England, Portugal, Prussia, Savoy and the United Provinces, Louis XIV allies with Spain and Bavaria

1702 Anne Stuart succeeds her brother-in-law William III as Queen of England, Scotland and Ireland

1703 St Petersburg founded by Tsar Peter the Great

1704 England conquers Gibraltar with Dutch support

1705 Tunisia breaks away from the Ottoman Turks

1707 'Acts of Union' Kingdoms of England, Scotland and Ireland jointed into the United Kingdom of Great Britain (UK)

1709 'Battle of Malplaquet (Mons, Fr.)' Main battle of the War of Spanish Succession; Lord Marlborough conducts the alliance to a Pyrrhic victory, the States Army of Prince John William Friso of Orange-Nassau suffers large losses

1709 Afghans proclaim their independence

1710 Mauritius in French hands; last Dodo killed

1710 Sir Christopher Wren, English architect, completes the rebuilding of *St Paul's Cathedral*, London

1711-1740 Reign of Charles VI of Austria, Holy Roman Emperor, has no male heir; 'Pragmatic Sanction' permits daughters to inherit, Holy Roman Empire is not divided

1712-1786 Life of King Frederick II (the Great) of Prussia, statesman, musician and philosopher

1713 'Treaty of Utrecht' ends the War of Spanish Succession; United Provinces set up fortresses in Spanish Netherlands

1713 'Asiento Contract' Great Britain obtains from Spain the slave trade from Africa to Spanish colonies in the Americas for the South Sea Company

Seven Provinces / Austrian Netherlands

1714 'Treaty of Rastatt (Ger.)' ends together with the Treaty of Utrecht, the hostilities between King Louis XIV of France and Charles VI of Austria; Austria obtains the southern Netherlands

1714 Elector of Hanover becomes George I, King of Great Britain and Ireland, after death of Queen Anne; first monarch of the House of Hanover

Low Countries

Wider World

1715 'Barrier-Treaty' United Provinces obtain the right to set up garrisons in Austrian Netherlands; closure of the Scheldt confirmed

1715 Louis XIV dies after a reign of 72 years; both King Louis XV and King Louis XVI continue the same decadent and prodigal life-style

1720-1889 'Middelburg (Zee.) Commercial Company (MCC)' operational; carries on, inter alia, the slave trade

1720-1911 Manchu Emperors of Qing dynasty govern Tibet, using Dalai Lama governors

1721 'Treaty of Nystad (Fin.)' Last peace treaty of the Great Northern War, concluded between the Russian and Swedish Empires

1722-1773 'Ostend (W. Flan.) East India Company' operational; competitor of VOC, WIC and MCC

1725 Jonathan Swift, Anglo-Irish essayist and satirist, completes *Gulliver's Travels*

1725 Antonio Vivaldi, Venetian violist and priest, composes *The Four Seasons*

1727 Great Britain and United Provinces press Emperor Charles VI of Austria to dissolve the Ostend East India Company

1728 Johann Sebastian Bach, German composer of baroque music and progenitor of the Bach generation, composes *St Matthew Passion*

1729-1751 William IV of Orange-Nassau, Stadtholder of Drenthe, Gelderland and Groningen

1730 Sodomy trials in Utrecht

1731-1751 William IV of Orange-Nassau, Stadtholder of Friesland

1733-1738 'War of Polish Succession' fought over the succession of Augustus II, King of Poland; widens as France and Spain attempt to check the power of the Austrian Habsburgs

1738 'Treaty of Vienna' Austria and Russia place Augustus III on Polish throne
1740 Frederick the Great conquers Silesia (Pol.) from Austria; introduces reforms

'Mit der Dummheit kämpfen die Götter selbst vergebens'
'Against stupidity even the Gods fight in vain', QUOTATION FROM FRIEDRICH SCHILLER, GERMAN POET, REGULARLY USED BY FREDERICK THE GREAT

1740-1748 'War of Austrian Succession' Charles VII of Bavaria, Philip V of Spain and Augustus III of Poland dispute succession of Maria Theresa of Austria
1740-1780 Reign of Maria Theresa, Archduchess of Austria; the only governing female monarch of the Habsburg House
1741 Vitus Bering, Danish navigator, explores at the request of Peter the Great of Russia the unchartered waters between America and Asia; discovers Alaska and the Bering Strait
1742 George Frideric Handel, German-English baroque composer, famous for his *Messiah*

1747 French irruption into the United Provinces; States-Flanders (Zee.) and Bergen op Zoom (N. Bra.) in French hands
1747 End of the Second Period without Stadtholder; William IV becomes Hereditary Stadtholder of the United Provinces, female succession made possible
1747 William IV moves his court from Leeuwarden (Frl.) to The Hague

1748 'Treaty of Aix-la-Chapelle (Ger.)' ends the War of Austrian Succession; Maria Theresa of Austria maintains control over the Austrian Netherlands

1750 VOC takes possession of Malacca and controls together with Maluku and Sunda the spice trade; blow to Venetian merchants

Low Countries	Wider World
	1751-1757 Marquis de Pombal, Prime Minister of Portugal; introduces reforms
1751-1795 Reign of William V of Orange-Nassau, the last Hereditary Stadtholder of the United Provinces; initially with a long Regency of four different Regents until 1766	
	1754-1763 'French and Indian War' Colonial war between France and Great Britain in North America and India
	1754-1838 Life of Charles-Maurice de Talleyrand, French diplomat and opportunistic politician under Louis XVI, Napoleon I, Louis XVIII, Charles X and Louis-Philippe
	1755 Earthquake in Lisbon; claims thirty thousand lives
	1756-1763 'Seven Years' War' pits Prussia, Great Britain and a coalition of smaller German states against an alliance of Austria, France, Russia, Saxony and Sweden; because of its global nature, due to the French and Indian War in the colonies, considered as the first World War
	1757 'Battle of Plassey (India)' Lord Robert Clive, Governor General of EIC, defeats Nawab of Bengal and his French allies; establishes EIC rule over India
	1759 Voltaire (François-Marie Arouet), French writer and philosopher, completes his polemic *Candide ou l'Optimisme*

'...mais il faut cultiver notre jardin'
'... but we should cultivate our garden', VOLTAIRE

Low Countries	Wider World
	1762-1796 Catherine (the Great), after engineering a military coup, becomes Tsarina of Russia
1763 Amsterdam bank De Neufville bankrupt; first international financial crisis	

1763 'Treaty of Paris' ends the French and Indian War and the Seven Years' War; France loses its colonies in India and North America, Great Britain obtains Canada, India, Florida and Louisiana, marks the beginning of an extensive period of British dominance outside Europe

1763 'Treaty of Hubertusburg (Ger.)' signed separately by Austria, Prussia and Saxony in conjunction with the Treaty of Paris; Silesia (Pol.) remains Prussian, so Prussia reaches the ranks of the great powers

1764 James Hargreaves, English weaver and inventor, develops the Spinning Jenny machine

1765 Wolfgang Amadeus Mozart, Austrian infant prodigy and composer, performs at the court of William V in The Hague

'The famous musician Wolfgang Mozart, but eight years old, executes most difficult compositions, as well as his own compositions'
LEYDEN JOURNAL

1765-1790 Joseph II, Holy Roman Emperor, rules the Austrian Netherlands together with Maria Theresa of Hungary until her death in 1789; enlightened absolutism

1768-1779 James Cook, English explorer, sails around Australia

1769 James Watt, Scottish inventor and engineer, develops the steam engine

'I sell here, Sir, what the entire world desires to have – power'
MATHEW BOULTON OF THE WATT BOULTON STEAM FACTORY

1769-1821 Life of Napoleon Bonaparte, Corsican military and political leader, head of state of France

From 1770 'Commonwealth of Nations' International organisation of independent member states, headed by the British monarch; forms the British Empire
1770-1831 Life of Georg Wilhelm Frederich Hegel, German philosopher, one of the creators of German Idealism

'Sein und Nichts sei dasselbe'
'*Being and non-being are the same*', Hegel

1772 'First Polish Partition' Austria, Prussia and Russia take first step in breaking up the Polish-Lithuanian Commonwealth
1773 'Boston Tea Party' Action by colonists in Boston, Mass. (US) against British trade acts; key event in the growth of the American Revolution
1773-1859 Life of Klemens, Prince von Metternich, Austrian politician and Chairman of Vienna Congress
1774 'First Continental Congress' Twelve of the thirteen North American colonies meet at Philadelphia, Penn. (US); onset of American Revolution
1774-1792 Reign of Louis XVI, King of France, married to Marie Antoinette, Archduchess of Austria; their joint prodigality leads to Revolution
1775-1783 'American Revolutionary War' Thirteen colonies in North America join together to break free from the British Empire; become the United States of America (US)

'We hold these truths to be self-evident, that all men are created equal: That they are endowed by their Creator with certain unalienable rights; that among these are life, liberty and the pursuit of happiness'
Declaration of Independence, 1776

1776 Edward Gibbon, English historian, writes *Decline and Fall of the Roman Empire*

Low Countries

1778 Patriots launch an unsuccessful coup in the United Provinces

1780-1784 'Fourth Anglo-Dutch War' Disagreement on the conduct of Dutch trade with Britain's enemies during the American Revolutionary War

1780-1795 Patriotic free corps emerge; crisis in the United Provinces

1781 'Patent of Tolerance' provides limited freedom of worship in the Austrian Netherlands

1781 Eise Eisinga, Frisian astronomer, builds first planetarium in his house in Franeker (Frl.); it still functions today

1785 Barrier Treaty withdrawn; Scheldt remains closed

1785 States of Holland limit powers of Stadtholder over the army; William V of Orange and Princess consort Wilhelmina of Prussia escape to the province of Gelderland

Wider World

1776 Adam Smith, Scottish moral philosopher and pioneer of political economics, writes *The Wealth of Nations*; defends free market economy

1780-1783 'First League of Armed Neutrality' Alliance of minor European naval powers to protect neutral shipping against British search of ships for contraband

1782 Ireland obtains virtual legislative independence from Great Britain; however, British government retains the right to nominate government of Ireland

1783 Russia annexes the Crimea (Ukr.) and establishes Georgia as a protectorate

1783-1830 Life of Simón Bolívar, Venezuelan military and political leader, plays key role in Hispanic American struggle for independence from the Spanish Empire; Bolivia, Columbia, Equador, Panama, Peru and Venezuela emerge

Low Countries

Wider World

1786 Wolfgang Amadeus Mozart, Austrian classical composer, writes the opera *The Marriage of Figaro*

1787 Patriots apprehend Princess Wilhelmina at Goejanverwellesluis (S. Hol.); her brother Frederick William II, King of Prussia, comes to her aid, drives off the Patriots and restores Stadtholder's authority

1787 Constitution of the United States of America ratified; first democratic constitution with separation of legislative, executive and judicial powers (*Trias Politica)*
1788 Prison colony Botany Bay in Sydney (Aus.) founded; beginning of colonisation and genocide of Aborigines

Modernisation

1789 Patriots in The Netherlands call for democratic rights

1789 'Tennis Court Oath' Third Estate signs a pledge in a tennis court in Paris; demanding a new constitution for France
1789 'Storming of Bastille' Mob storms the Bastille prison in Paris; insurrection and spirit of popular sovereignty spreads throughout France
1789 'Declaration of Rights of Man and Citizen' published by French National Assembly; comprises statement of principles, rather than constitution with legal effects
1789-1797 George Washington, Commander of the Continental Army, serves as the first President of the United States of America

1790 Union of Liberals and Clericals against the reforms of Joseph II; entices the southern Netherlands to proclaim the United Belgian States

Low Countries

1790 Bishopric Principality of Liège revises its civic rights in line with the French model
1790 Austria restores its authority over the southern Netherlands

1792 French troops invade the Austrian Netherlands
1792-1795 Francis II, Holy Roman Emperor, rules the Austrian Netherlands

1793 Austria restores once again its authority over the southern Netherlands

1794 'Battle of Fleurus (Hain.)' French Army defeats Coalition Army; leads to permanent loss of the southern Netherlands by Austria to the French and ushers the ending of the United Provinces

Wider World

1791 Proclamation of French Constitution; France becomes a constitutional monarchy
1792 National Assembly declares France a republic and abolishes the monarchy; Louis XVI deposed

1792-1797 'War of the First Coalition' France at war with Austria, Great Britain, Portugal, Prussia, Spain, United Provinces and some Italian states; first coalition to contain Revolutionary France
1792-1815 'French Revolutionary Wars' Series of conflicts between Revolutionary France and several successive and differently composed European coalitions

1793 Louis XVI guillotined
1793 'Second Polish Partition' Prussia and Russia continue the break-up of the Polish-Lithuanian Commonwealth
1793-1794 'Reign of Terror' stimulated by Maximilien Robespierre, one of the best-known and most influential figures of the French Revolution

Batavian Republic / First French Republic

1795 'Batavian Revolution' With help of the French Revolutionary Army under general Charles Pichegru, and aided by frozen rivers, Patriots take control; Stadtholder Willem V flees to England
1795 Slave rebellion at Curaçao (Dutch Antilles), with Tula as their leader

1795 'Third Polish Partition' Austria, Prussia and Russia complete division of the Polish-Lithuanian Commonwealth
1795 'Peace of Basel' France makes peace with Prussia, Spain and Hesse-Kassel; these countries revoke their alliance with Austria
1795 Great Britain occupies the Dutch colony on the shores of the Table Bay (S. Afr.)
1795-1799 'Directory' More moderate administration of five Directors in France; constitutes the last stage of the French Revolution
1796 Edward Jenner, English scientist, develops smallpox vaccine
1797 Napoleon conducts successful campaign against Austria in Italy; Republic of Venice loses its independence, after 1070 years

1796 First Dutch elections for the National Assembly of the Batavian Republic; next Dutch general elections take place nearly 100 years later
1797 'Peace of Campo Formio (It.)' Victorious campaigns in Italy mark collapse of the First Coalition; Austrian Netherlands, Bouillon and Bishopric Principality of Liège annexed by France

1797 Johann von Goethe, German writer and polymath, publishes his magnum opus, the tragedy *Faust*

'Von Zeit zu Zeit seh ich den Alten gern, und hüte mich, mit ihm zu brechen. Es ist gar hübsch von einem großen Herrn, so menschlich mit dem Teufel selbst zu sprechen'

' From time to time I like to see the Old Man, but take care not to break with him, It is quite nice for a great Lord, so human to speak with the devil himself '

DEVIL MEPHISTOPHOLES, IN FAUST

1798 VOC dissolved, after nearly three centuries

1798 Jean Pierre Minckelers, Dutch natural philosopher, inventor of illuminating gas

1798 Joseph Haydn, Austrian prolific classical composer, completes *The Creation*

1798 'Battle of the Nile' Lord Nelson defeats French fleet near Abukir (Egyp.), Napoleon's Army trapped in Egypt; encourages European countries to turn on France and form the 'Second Coalition'

1798 Thomas Robert Malthus, English scholar in political economy, writes *An Essay on the Principle of Population;* popularises the economic theory of rent

1798-1802 'War of the Second Coalition' Second attempt to eliminate Revolutionary France; led by Austria and Russia, with help of Great Britain, Naples, Portugal and Turkey

1799 French expeditionary force in Egypt finds the *Rosetta Stone* with three texts: hieroglyphs, Demotic and Greek; provides key to deciphering ancient hieroglyphs

1799-1804 Napoleon overthrows French Directory and becomes First Consul

1800 Malta becomes a British Dominion

1800 'Battle of Marengo (Piemonte, It.)' Napoleon drives the Austrians out of Italy; enhances his position in Paris

From 1800 Industrialisation of England starts

1800-1801 'Second League of Armed Neutrality' Alliance of Denmark, Prussia, Sweden and Russia to prevent Great Britain interfering with their neutral shipping

1801 'Battle of Copenhagen' British fleet under Admiral Sir Hyde Parker defeats a Danish-Norwegian fleet; Lord Nelson leads the attack, disobeying Parker's order to withdraw

1801 'Treaty of Lunéville (Fr.)' signed between France and Austria, marks the end of the Second Coalition; Great Britain remains the sole nation at war with France, France obtains the old 'limes' (Alps, Pyrenees, Rhine) which Julius Caesar gave to the Gauls

1801-1805 'State Council' Governing council of the Batavian Republic; its Presidents act as head of state

1801-1825 Tsar Alexander I (the Blessed) of Russia; carries out legal and social reforms

1803 Robert Fulton, American engineer and inventor, develops the first successful steamboat; steams first on the Seine (Fr.), then on the Hudson (US)

1803-1814 'War between Britain and France' Protected by the navy Britain maintains low-intensity land warfare on a global scale

'I do not say. my Lords, that the French will not come.
I say only they will not come by sea'
ADMIRAL JERVIS TO THE HOUSE OF LORDS

1804 Richard Trevithick, Cornish inventor and mining engineer, develops a steam engine and builds the first working steam locomotive

1804 Napoleon I crowns himself the first Emperor of the French since Charlemagne, in the presence of the Pope

Batavian Republic / First French Empire

1804-1814 First French Empire; Bonaparte dynasty established

1805 Napoleon I makes Rutger Jan Schimmelpenninck, Dutch politician, Grand Pensionary and sole ruler of the Batavian Republic

1805 'Battle of Trafalgar (Sp.)' British fleet led by Admiral Nelson defeats the combined French and Spanish fleet; Admiral Nelson is fatally wounded

'England expects that every man will do his duty'
NELSON'S FLAG SIGNAL

1805 'Battle of Austerlitz (Czech.)' French Imperial Army destroys the Army of the Third Coalition (Austria, Britain, Portugal, Russia, Naples, Sicily and Sweden); Napoleon's greatest victory

1806 Britain occupies the Cape Colony to protect this Dutch-owned strategic point against the French; subsequently it remains in the British Empire

1806-1813 'Confederation of the Rhine' consists of thirty-five Principalities of the eastern German part of the Holy Roman Empire, which become client states of the First French Empire; leads to the end of the Holy Roman Empire

1806 Francis II abdicates, thus ending the Holy Roman Empire after nearly 1000 years; continues as Emperor of Austria and King of Hungary

'The Holy Roman Empire was neither Holy, nor Roman, nor an Empire'
VOLTAIRE IS SUPPOSED TO HAVE SAID

Kingdom of Holland / First French Empire

1806 Napoleon I appoints his brother Louis Bonaparte, King of Holland, and his niece and Louis' wife, Hortense de Beauharnais, Queen of Holland

'Ik ben Konijn van Holland'
'I be Cony of Holland',
King Louis, trying to speak Dutch, uses Cony instead of King'

1807 'Second Battle of Copenhagen' Pre-emptive British attack on the city to seize the Dano-Norwegian fleet; forces King Frederick VI of Denmark and Norway into an alliance with Napoleon I
1807 'Slave Trade Act' After having transported half of the number of slaves to the Americas, Britain now abolishes slave trade in the British Empire; slavery itself not abolished until 1833
1807-1813 Napoleon I establishes the Duchy of Warsaw, from Polish land obtained from Prussia and Austria after their Polish Partitions
1808-1809 'Finnish War' fought between Sweden and Russia; eastern part of Sweden established as Grand Duchy of Finland
1808-1814 'Peninsular War' Contest between France and the Allied powers of Great Britain, Portugal and Spain for control of the Iberian Peninsula; brings about the struggle for independence of the Iberian colonies in southern America
1809 Napoleon I conquers Vienna; marries Marie Louise, daughter of Austrian Emperor Francis II in 1810
1809 British Army lands in Walcheren (Zee.) en route to Antwerp; first military use of rockets, developed by William Congreve, English engineer

c 1809 Islamic Fulani settle in the Hausa State (Nigeria); large Islamic Hausa-Fulani State emerges

First French Empire

1810 Kingdom of Holland becomes part of the First French Empire, just like the southern Netherlands earlier; Napoleonic Code (French civil code) established
1811-1816 England assumes power over Netherlands East Indies, Sir Thomas Raffles, English statesman, appointed Lieutenant-Governor; land tenure system introduced

1812 Napoleon's Army retreats from Moscow with a loss of five hundred thousand men; triggers 'War of the Sixth Coalition (Austria, Britain, Prussia, Russia and Sweden)' against France
1812-1814 'Anglo-American War' fought between the forces of the US and the UK; conquest of British Canada by the US prevented
1813 Prussia changes position and declares war on France
1813 Jane Austen, English novelist, publishes her famous work of romantic fiction *Pride and Prejudice*

'It is a truth universally acknowledged, that a single man in possession of a good fortune, must be in want of a wife'
JANE AUSTEN

1813 'Battle of the Nations' Sixth Coalition (Austria, Britain, Portugal, Prussia, Spain, Russia, Sweden and smaller German States) battles with France and Saxons near Leipzig (Ger.); Napoleon is defeated after the Saxons desert him

1813 French forces leave the northern Netherlands, William Frederick, Prince of Orange-Nassau lands at Scheveningen (The Hague); Triumvirate (Van Hogendorp, Van Limburg Stirum and Van der Duyn van Maasdam) receive him in state as sovereign monarch

'Our Fatherland has been saved, good times will return soon'
PUBLIC ANNOUNCEMENT OF WILLIAM FREDERICK

1813 Mexico declares itself independent
1813-1907 'The Great Game' Conflict between British Empire and Russian Empire for supremacy in Central Asia
1814 Sixth Coalition forces occupy Paris; Napoleon I abdicates and is exiled to Elba (It.), Louis XVIII becomes King of France

1814 French forces leave southern Netherlands, William Frederick of Orange-Nassau becomes Regent
1814 Slave trade banned in The Netherlands under pressure from the British

1814-1815 'Congress of Vienna' Conference of ambassadors of Europe, chaired by Otto von Metternich; determines new boundaries in Europe, amongst which are those of the Low Countries

'Le congrès danse beaucoup, mais il ne marche pas'
'*The Congress dances a lot, but it does not walk*', ACCORDING TO PARTICIPANT PRINCE DE LIGNE

1815 Brazil declares itself independent
1815 'Hundred Days' Napoleon Bonaparte escapes from Elba, lands in southern France and returns as Emperor; Louis XVIII flees

1815 'Battle of Waterloo (Wal. Bra.)' Imperial Army under Napoleon I defeated by the combined Armies of the Seventh Coalition, under command of the Duke of Wellington, supported by the Prussian Army under command of Gebhard von Blücher; Crown Prince William of Orange-Nassau leads The Netherlands Army

'Ours is composed of the scum of the earth – the mere scum of the earth'
WELLINGTON ON HIS ARMY, BEFORE THE BATTLE

1815 Napoleon begins his exile on Saint Helena, a British island in the Atlantic Ocean

United Kingdom of The Netherlands

1815 United Kingdom of The Netherlands formed from the United Provinces, the Austrian Netherlands and Bishopric Principality of Liège; forms with Grand Duchy of Luxembourg a buffer state against France
1815 The Netherlands maintains two governmental centres Brussels and The Hague; alternating every year

1815-1824 King Louis XVIII reigns again in France

1815-1840 Reign of William I, King of the United Kingdom of The Netherlands and Grand Duke of Luxembourg

1815-1866 'German Confederation' Association of forty-one Central European states acts as successor to the Holy Roman Empire; maintains German unity

1816 The Netherlands regain authority over Netherlands East Indies
1817 Botanic garden set up at Buitenzorg, near Batavia (Netherlands East Indies)

1818 Chile declares itself independent

1818-1844 Jean Baptiste Bernadotte, Marshal of France, reigns as Charles XIV John, King of Sweden and Norway

1819 Thomas Raffles establishes a trading settlement in Singapore

1820 Pierre Pelletier and Joseph Caventou, French biologists, use quinine against malaria

1821 Setting-up of the Gold Standard

1821 Mexico and Peru declare themselves independent

1821-1830 'Greek War of Independence' begins after the murder of the Patriarch of Constantinople by Sultan Mahmoud II of the Ottoman Empire; Greeks obtain assistance from several European states

1822 Eugène Delacroix, French romantic painter, depicts in *Massacre of Chios* (Gr.) the horrors carried out on the island by the Ottoman Empire; causes a wave of outrage against the Turks in Europe

1823 Ludwig van Beethoven, German pianist and famous composer, completes his 9th Symphony *Ode to Joy*

'All humans become brothers'
EUROPEAN ANTHEM

1824 'Anglo-Dutch Treaty' resolves issues that arose during the British occupation of Dutch possessions in Asia during the Napoleonic Wars; England keeps Singapore and Malacca, The Netherlands obtain Sumatra

1824 Lord Byron, English poet and leading figure in Romanticism, dies in Misolóngi (Gr.); draws attention to the Greek War of Independence by his local presence

1824-1826 'First Anglo-Burmese War' Burma cedes swaths of territory, pays indemnity

1824-1830 Charles X, King of France

1825-1830 'Java War' Javanese aristocrats rebel against Dutch predominance in Netherlands East Indies

1825-1855 Reign of Nicolas I, Tsar of Russia

1827 Franz Schubert, Austrian composer, famous for his *Winterreise*

1827 'Battle of Navarino (Ionian Sea)' Combined Ottoman and Egyptian fleet destroyed by combined British, French and Russian fleet during the Greek War of Independence

1829 Nathaniel Wyeth, American inventor, patents a production process for ice-making; to keep and transport frozen food

1829 George Stephenson, English inventor, develops steam engine *The Rocket*

1830 'July Revolution' Charles X, last king of the Bourbon monarchy replaced by his cousin Louis-Philippe I of Orleans (the Citizen King)

1830 Union of Liberals and Clericals forms the revolutionary movement in Brussels, as in 1790

1830 Performance of the opera *The Mute Girl of Portici* causes an insurrection in Brussels

'Amour sacrée de la patrie'

'*Holy patriotic love*', ARIA FROM PORTICI

1830 Charles Babbage, English mathematician and inventor, invents the first programmable mechanical calculator; father of the computer

1830 France invades the Ottoman province of Algeria

1830 Provisional Government in Brussels declares creation of the independent State of Belgium, in revolt against the United Kingdom of The Netherlands; National Congress votes for a parliamentary hereditary monarchy

1830 'London Conference' imposes an armistice between Belgium and The Netherlands; border of 1790 is dividing line between the armies

From 1830 Industrialisation of Belgium starts

1830-1831 'Polish November Uprising' Armed rebellion against the Russian Empire in Belarus, Lithuania, Poland and Ukraine; crushed by a numerically superior Russian Army, supported by the Prussians

1830-1870 Cultivation System introduced in Netherlands East Indies; native people must cultivate agricultural products for European markets

1830-1899 Life of Guido Gezelle, Flemish priest and influential Flemish language writer

1831 'London Conference' announces the basis for the separation; XVIII articles determine the separation of Belgium and The Netherlands

1831 National Congress agrees to a liberal constitution for Belgium; general freedom of language, legal courts and institutions choose French, also for Flemish-speaking provinces

1831 Orangistic conspiracies in Antwerp and Ghent (E. Fla.)

1831 Jan van Speijk, Dutch naval officer, runs aground in the river Scheldt; blows up his ship rather than let it fall into Belgian hands

'Rather into the air…'

Van Speijk, throwing his burning cigar into the open gunpowder barrel

Kingdom of Belgium / Kingdom of The Netherlands

1831 Belgium becomes an independent Kingdom

Low Countries

1831 National Congress accepts the XVIII articles; however, wishes to maintain the borders of 1790, the addition of Limburg and Luxembourg to Belgium and free access to the river Scheldt

1831 King Leopold I of Belgium declares Limburg and Luxembourg part of Belgium

1831 'Ten Days Campaign' Failed attempt to suppress the Belgian revolution by William I; Dutch Army invades Belgium, France Army supports the Belgians, Prussian and Russian help to the Dutch not forthcoming due to the Polish Uprising

1831 London Conference replaces the XVIII articles by XXIV articles; declares Limburg and Luxembourg as belonging to Belgium

1831-1865 Reign of Leopold I, Prince of Saxe-Coburg-Gotha, as King of the Belgians

1832 Leopold I marries Louise-Marie of Orleans, daughter of the French King Louis-Philippe I

1832 Dutch Army evacuates the Citadel of Antwerp

1834 Dissension in The Netherlands Reformed Church; independent Calvinistic churches arise

Wider World

1831 French Foreign Legion founded

1831 Michael Faraday, English chemist and physicist, discovers electromagnetic induction

1831 Sir James Clark Ross, English naval officer and explorer, locates the position of the Magnetic North Pole

1832 Greece recognised as sovereign nation by the Ottoman Empire; Prince Otto van Wittelsbach, King of Greece

1833-1876 'Carlist Wars' Last European civil wars fought to establish claims to the throne of Spain; leaves the country divided

1834 Slavery is abolished in most of the British Empire; with the exception of the territories of Ceylon, EIC and St Helena

1835 First train on the European Continent, travels from Brussels to Mechlin (Antw.)

1835-1837 'Great Trek' Boers migrate eastward and north-eastward, away from British control in the Cape Colony (S. Afr.)
1836 Charles Dickens, English novelist, popular for his iconic characters, starts his book *The Pickwick Papers*
1836 'Battle of the Alamo' and 'Battle of San Jacinto' Pivotal and decisive battles between Mexico and the State of Texas during the 'Texas Revolution'
1837-1901 *Victorian Era* Queen Victoria reigns over the UK for nearly 64 years; period of industrial, cultural, political, scientific and military progress
1838 Samuel Morse, American painter and inventor, completes the electric telegraph system

'... — — — ...'
SAVE OUR SOULS

1839 First railroad in The Netherlands between Amsterdam and Haarlem (N. Hol.)
1839 'First Treaty of London' Peace between Belgium and The Netherlands, William I signs the XXIV articles; Limburg divided between Belgium and The Netherlands, Luxembourg partly to Belgium, Belgium pays for sailing rights through the Scheldt

1839-1842 'First Opium War' British Empire against China under the Qing dynasty; beginning of European hegemony in China

1839-1842 'First Anglo-Afghan War' ends with Afghan victory and British withdrawal

1840 First British colonists reach New Zealand; founding of Wellington

1840-1849 Reign of William II, King of The Netherlands, Grand Duke of Luxembourg

1840-1889 Life of Flemish Father Damiaan, worked with lepers; canonised and voted *The Greatest Belgian* at the beginning of the 21st century

1842 'Treaty of Nanking' marks the end of the First Opium War; establishes Hong Kong as a British colony

1842 'Belgian-Netherlands Treaty' settles demarcation of the borders and payment for use of the Scheldt

1843 Sir Charles Napier, British general, conquers the Sindh Province (Pak.) in India

1844 Setting-up of the Gold Standard in the UK

1844 France brings Morocco under control

1844-1900 Life of Friedrich Nietzsche, German philosopher and philologist, wrote with fondness for metaphor and irony *Also sprach Zarathustra* (Thus spoke Zarathustra)

'Was mich nicht umbringt, macht mich stärker'
'*If it does not kill me, it makes me stronger*', NIETZSCHE

1845-1852 *Great Famine* Period of mass starvation and disease in Ireland; mass emigration to the US

1846-1848 'Mexican-American War' between the US and Mexico in the wake of the US annexation of Texas in 1845; Mexico forced to sell its northern territories to the US

1847 Liberia, second independent republic founded by former slaves in West Africa

1848 Karl Marx and Friedrich Engels, both German philosophers, finish the *Communist Manifesto*; lays out the Communist League's programme, a most influential political publication

'Proletarier aller Länder vereinigt euch!'
'*Workers of the world, unite!*', MARX & ENGELS

1848 Monarchy abolished in France; Second Republic with Louis Napoleon Bonaparte, cousin of Napoleon I and son of Hortense de Beauharnais, as President

1848 France demands annexation of Belgium and extension of the French border to the river Rhine; rapprochement between Belgium and The Netherlands
1848 William II accepts proposal of Johan Rudolf Thorbecke, Dutch Liberal statesman, for revision of the Constitution; leading principle *The King is inviolable, the Ministers are responsible*

1848 Failed attempt to bring unity to Germany by means of a Parliament in Frankfurt
1848 John Stuart Mill, English philosopher and civil servant, publishes *The Principles of Political Economy*
1848-1849 'First Italian War of Independence' fought between the Kingdom of Piedmont-Sardinia and the Austrian Empire; Austrians under Josef Radetzky, Czech nobleman, manage to defeat the Piedmonts; defeat immortalized by Johan Strauss, Austrian composer, in the *Radetzky March*
1848-1861 'Il Risorgimento' Italian unification, political and social movement accomplished by Benzo Cavour, Giuseppe Garibaldi, Daniele Manin and Giuseppe Mazinni
1848-1916 Emperor Franz Joseph I rules Austria-Hungary

Low Countries | Wider World

1849-1890 William III, King of The Netherlands and Grand Duke of Luxembourg

1850 Gold rush in Australia stimulates further development
From 1850 Industrialisation of Europe and the US takes off
1850-1865 'Taiping Rebellion' Civil war in southern China, led by heterodox Christian Hong Xiuquan against the ruling Qing dynasty; one of the deadliest conflicts in Chinese history
1851 Giuseppe Verdi, Italian romantic composer, writes his magnum opus *Rigoletto*
1852 'Sand River Convention' Great Britain recognises the independence of the Boers living beyond the Vaal river; slavery outlawed

'O bring me back to the old Transvaal, there where my Sary lives'
DUTCH-AFRICAN FOLK-SONG

1852-1853 'Second Anglo-Burmese War' Province of Pegu annexed by Great Britain
1852-1870 Louis-Napoleon Bonaparte III, Emperor of the Second French Empire

1853 Leopold II, Prince of Belgium, marries Marie Henriette of Austria

1853-1856 'Crimean War' between Russia and an alliance of the French Empire, British Empire, Ottoman Empire and the Kingdom of Sardinia for influence over the declining Ottoman Empire; Florence Nightingale (*Lady with the Lamp*) faces many dangers to offer medical aid to the soldiers

'The first requirement in a hospital is that it should do the sick no harm'
FLORENCE NIGHTINGALE

1854 Republican Party founded in the US; advocates anti-slavery and protective import duties

1854 'Contract of Bloemfontein' Great Britain recognises independence of Orange Free State, while Natal is annexed

1854 US Commodore Matthew Perry forces Japan to open its ports to foreign traders

1855-1881 Tsar Alexander II of Russia starts a period of reforms

1856 Sir Henry Bessemer, English engineer, invents the Bessemer process for manufacturing steel; later improved by the German-born engineer Sir Charles William Siemens and the French engineer Pierre-Émile Martin

1856 Definite reconciliation between Belgium and The Netherlands; new Dutch text of the Brabançonne, the Belgian National Anthem

1856-1860 'Second Opium War' pits the British Empire with the Second French Empire against the Qing dynasty; Beijing occupied, Summer Palace destroyed

1856–1877 Transvaal and Orange Free State form the South African Republic, an independent Boer-ruled country

1857 Gustave Flaubert, French writer, completes his famous first novel *Madame Bovary*

1857 'Indian Rebellion' Mutinies and civilian rebellions against EIC; ends EIC's rule in India, Viceroy appointed

1858 'Treaty of Tianjin' ends the Second Opium War; legalises import of opium into China, permits foreign legations in Beijing, allows Christian missionary activities

1858-1862 French occupy Indo-China

1859 Charles Darwin, English naturalist, describes his evolution theory in *On the Origin of Species*

'I have called this principle, by which each slight variation, if useful, is preserved, by the term of Natural Selection'

Darwin

1859 'Second War of Italian Independence' fought by Napoleon III of France and the Kingdom of Piedmont-Sardinia against the Austrian Empire

1859 'Battle of Solferino (It.)' results in a victory of the joint French and Piedmont Armies against the Austrian Army, turning point in the Resorgimento; cruelties perpetrated lead to the Geneva Convention and the Red Cross

1860 Vladivostok founded in Siberia (Rus.)

1860 'i Mille (the Thousand)' Giuseppe Garibaldi, Italian patriot, gathers one thousand volunteers, sails to Sicily and southern Italy to add these areas to the Italian Kingdom

1860 Eduard Douwes Dekkers (pen-name Multatuli), Dutch writer, publishes the satirical novel *Max Havelaar*; denounces abuses of colonialism in Netherlands East Indies

'I am a trader in coffee and live at 37 Lauriergracht'
FIRST PHRASE MAX HAVELAAR

1860 Flemish movement puts the language problem in Belgium on the political agenda

1861 Republican Abraham Lincoln elected President of the United States of America; eleven southern slave states set up the Confederate States of America

1861 Tsar Alexander II abolishes serfdom for forty-five million peasants in Russia

1861-1865 'American Civil War' between the (southern) Confederate States and the (northern) United States

1861-1878 Reign of Victor Emmanuel II, King of Italy

1862 Richard Gatling, American inventor, develops a machine gun with multi-barrel design

1862 Victor Hugo, French poet and statesman, releases his most famous novel *Les Misérables*

1862-1890 Otto von Bismarck, German statesman, Prime Minister of Prussia; oversees the unification of Germany

1863 Slavery abolished in Surinam and the Netherlands Antilles

1863 Shipping rights on the river Scheldt granted; Belgium pays 440,000 guilders a year

1863 British and American settlements in Shanghai merge into the Shanghai International Settlement; with special arrangements for westerners

1863 Henri Dunant, Swiss banker, sets up the International Committee of the Red Cross in Geneva

1863 'Battle of Gettysburg, Penn. (US)' Union Army defeats the Confederate Army; President Lincoln announces liberation of slaves

1863-1872 Pieter Caland, Dutch engineer of Public Works, plans and completes the New Waterway; which joins Rotterdam without locks or bridges with the North Sea

1864 'Geneva Convention' sets standards for humanitarian treatment of victims of war

1864 'Danish-Prussian War' Military conflict over succession of the Duchies of Schleswig and Holstein, which go to Prussia; first of three wars which lead to the German Empire

1864 Louis Pasteur, French chemist and microbiologist, invents pasteurisation; method to sterilise milk and wine to prevent illness

1865 President Lincoln of the United States of America murdered

1865 Confederate Armies surrender to the Union Army throughout North America

1865-1877 'Reconstruction' African-Americans in the United States obtain voting rights, which civil servants sabotage

1865-1909 Reign of Leopold II, King of the Belgians

1866 'Austro-Prussian War' fought between the German Confederation and the Kingdoms of Prussia and Italy; results in Prussian dominance over German States, second war leading to the German Empire

1866 Alfred Nobel, Swedish chemist and armaments manufacturer, patents dynamite, his major invention

1866-1868 Introduction of the parliamentary system in The Netherlands

1866-1871 'North German Confederation' Military alliance of 22 states in northern Germany with the Kingdom of Prussia as leading state, organised by Otto von Bismarck; leads to the German Empire

1867 Typewriter invented by Sholes, Glidden and Soule and commercialised by Remington

1867 'British North America Act' Canada, first dominion of Great Britain, formed by royal assent

1867 Karl Marx writes and Friedrich Engels edits in part the book *Capital*; critical analysis of capitalism

1867-1918 Emperor Franz Joseph I keeps Hungary on equal footing with Austria; double monarchy Austria-Hungary

1867 'Luxembourg Crisis' France offers to buy Luxembourg from William III; Otto von Bismarck calls it a *casus bellli* (reason for war)

1867 'Second Treaty of London' Luxembourg remains patrimonial property of the House of Orange-Nassau; but becomes politically neutral

1868 'Meiji Restoration' restores power from the Tokugawa shogunate and gives it back to the Emperor; westernisation and use of economic growth factors, such as education and market economy, starts

1868 'Treaty of Mannheim' International agreement among the bordering states, which regulates the traffic on the river Rhine

1869 Count Leo Tolstoy, Russian writer, completes his masterpiece *War and Peace*
1869 Suez Canal opened, which connects the Mediterranean Sea with the Red Sea, developed by the French diplomat Viscount Ferdinand de Lesseps; reduces sailing time between West and East
1869-1948 Life of Mahatma Gandhi (Great Soul), lawyer and spiritual leader of India during the Indian independence movement; uses civil disobedience based on non-violence

'On this world there is enough for people's need, but not enough for people's greed'
Gandhi

1870 Agricultural law established in Netherlands East Indies; European private entrepreneurs permitted

1870 Rome becomes the capital of Italy, Pope retreats into the Vatican; Dogma of Papal infallibility
1870 'Franco-Prussian War' between France and Prussia, aided by the North German Federation and the southern German states of Baden, Württemberg and Bavaria; complete victory at Sedan (Fr.) under King Wilhelm I of Prussia brings about the final unification of Germany

1870 King Wilhelm I of Prussia proclaimed Emperor Wilhelm I of Germany in Versailles (Fr.); Emperor Louis Napoleon III of France is deposed, Third Republic declared in France, cession of Alsace-Lorraine to the German Empire

From 1870 Industrialisation of The Netherlands starts

1870-1890 Otto von Bismarck first Chancellor of the German Empire
1871 Diamonds found near Kimberly (S. Africa)
1872 Elmina (Ghana), centre of the slave trade of the WIC, handed over to the UK
1872 Leo Tolstoy, completes another masterpiece *Anna Karenina*
1872 Henry Morton Stanley, Welsh journalist and explorer, locates missing Scottish explorer and missionary, Dr. David Livingstone, in Ujiji, near Lake Tanganyika (Tanzania)

'Dr. Livingstone, I presume?'
STANLEY

1873 Members of the Latin Monetary Union (Belgium, France, Italy, Switzerland) agree to change their national currencies to the Gold Standard and make them freely interchangeable

1873 *First Language Law* Dutch becomes the official language in Flemish Courts of Law
1873-1913 'Aceh War' Conflict with the Sultanate of Aceh (northern Sumatra), with the highest population of Muslims in Netherlands East Indies

1873-1887 'Three Emperors' League' Alliance of the Emperors of Austria-Hungary, Germany and Russia, arranged by Otto von Bismarck; aimed at neutralising rivalry over the Balkans and the isolation of France

1874 *Children Law of Van Houten* improves life of working children through advances in law and regulations in The Netherlands

1874-1880 *Second Disraeli Ministry* Benjamin Disraeli, Conservative statesman and literary figure, operates with absolute majority in the House of Commons; introduces various reforms

1875 Gold Standard established in The Netherlands

1875-1876 Revolt in the European Turkish area leads to the states of Bulgaria, Rumania and Serbia

1876 'Brussels Geographical Conference' First conference on the subject of colonising and exploring Central Africa, held in Brussels

'To open the only part of the world, where civilisation has not yet penetrated'
LEOPOLD II

1876 Richard Wagner, German composer and theatre director, performs his four-opera cycle *The Ring of the Nibelung* in Bayreuth (Ger.)
1876 Alexander Bell, Scottish scientist and engineer, invents and develops the telephone commercially

'Mr. Watson, come here, I want to see you…'
ALEXANDER BELL'S FIRST SUCCESSFUL CALL

1876 Queen Victoria of Great Britain takes the title of Empress of India
1876-1909 Sultan Abdul Hamid II rules with absolute power in the final period of decline of the Ottoman Empire, supported by the secret police
1877 Great Britain annexes the South African Republic

1878 *Second Language Law* arranges the use of languages in governmental matters in Brussels and Flanders

Low Countries

1878 Anti Revolutionary Party (ARP) established in The Netherlands by Abraham Kuyper, Dutch theologian and statesman

1879 Aletta Jacobs, first female physician in The Netherlands

1880 School quarrels between Roman Catholics and Liberals in Belgium
c 1880 Rotterdam develops into the world's biggest port

1880-1962 Life of Wilhelmina, Princess of Orange-Nassau
1881 Hendrik Willem Mesdag, Dutch painter creates the *Panorama Scheveningen*

Wider World

1878 Bosnia and Herzegovina occupied by Austria
1878 'Congress of Berlin' Meeting of Europe's great powers and Ottoman statesmen; Otto von Bismarck undertakes to balance the interests of Austria-Hungary, Russia and Great Britain
1878-1880 'Second Anglo-Afghan War' Afghans maintain internal sovereignty, cede control of foreign affairs to British goverment

1879 'Anglo-Zulu War' between British Empire and Zulu Empire under King Shaka; ends with Zulu nation's independence
1879 Thomas Edison, American inventor, scientist and businessman, patented many influential devices; tests successfully the electric light bulb

1880-1881 'First Anglo-Boer War' Boers from the Transvaal under Paul Kruger proclaim the South African Republic again
1881 'Pretoria Convention' gives Boers self-rule in the Transvaal and Orange Free State; under British sovereignty

1881 France occupies Tunisia
1881 Tsar Alexander II murdered
1881-1894 Reign of Tsar Alexander III; restores absolutism

1882 'Anglo-Egyptian War' British Expeditionary Force defeats the Egyptian Army; Egypt occupied, joint British-French management of the Suez Canal terminated
1882 Thomas Edison starts the first electrical power plant in New York
1882-1885 Gottlieb Daimler, German engineer and industrialist, invents the petrol engine and the first four-wheel automobile
1882-1898 'French-Samori War' between French Republic and Islamic Samori Empire; ends in defeat of Samori monarchy
1882-1914 'Triple Alliance' Military alliance between Germany, Austria-Hungary and Italy; members promise mutual support in the event of an attack

1883 *Third Language Law* Dutch in Flemish public schools, Roman Catholic secondary schools remain French speaking
1883 World Exhibition in Amsterdam; first international colonial and export exhibition, attracts over one million visitors
1883 De Khotinsky, Russian inventor, establishes the first electric light bulb factory in Rotterdam
1883 Krakatoa volcano erupts near Java, Netherlands East Indies; thirty-six thousand people killed

1884 Timisoara (then Austria-Hungary, now Romania) is the first European city with electric street lights
1884 'London Convention' restores the South African Republic with full independence
1884-1885 'Berlin Conference' organised by Otto von Bismarck, regulates European colonisation in Africa, which formalises the 'Scramble for Africa' among the West European States; Germany obtains mandate over Togo and Cameron, France protectorate over Annam and Tonkin

1885 King Leopold II buys for himself Congo Free State (Central Africa); manages it brutally as private enterprise
1885 Establishment of the Socialist Union in Belgium
1885 Vincent van Gogh, Dutch post-impressionist painter, completes his famous painting *The Potato Eaters*

1885 Karl Benz, German engine designer and engineer, regarded as the inventor of the gasoline-powered automobile; founder of Mercedes-Benz
1885 Russia attacks Afghanistan
1885 First electric tramway in Europe runs in Sarajevo (Bosn. & Herz.)
1885 Indian National Congress founded; largest and one of the oldest democratic parties in the world
1885-1886 'Third Anglo-Burmese War' ends the ruling dynasty; Burma under the rule of the British Raj
1885-1899 Cecil Rhodes, English mining magnate and Prime Minister of Cape Colony; takes possession for Britain of Botswana, Kenya, Uganda, Sudan, Somalia and Zimbabwe
1887 'Indo-China Union' Federation of Vietnam, Cambodia and Laos; consolidates French position in East Asia
1887-1890 'Reinsurance Treaty' Secret agreement between Germany and Russia, arranged by Otto von Bismarck; ensures reciprocal neutrality
1887-1890 Italy occupies Eritrea (East Africa)
1888-1918 Reign of Wilhelm II, Emperor of Germany
1889 Brazil abolishes the monarchy and declares itself a republic
1889 Division of Somalia (East Africa) between Italy and UK

Belgium / Luxembourg / The Netherlands

1890 King William III dies, Salic Law allows only male heirs; Grand Duchess of Luxembourg brings the House of Nassau-Welburg to the throne

1890 Otto von Bismarck dismissed; Reinsurance Treaty terminated

'Einer Tag der große Europäische Krieg werd entstehen aus eine Verdammte Dummheit in der Balkan'

'One day the great European War will come out from some damned foolish thing in the Balkans'
PREDICTED BY BISMARCK AT THE TIME OF HIS DISMISSAL, 24 YEARS BEFORE WW I

1890 Gold discovered near Witwatersrand (S. Afr.); influx of non-Boer European settlers (Outlanders) destabilises the South African Republic
1890 'Helgoland (Ger.) - Zanzibar Treaty' Agreement between UK and Germany concerning territorial interests in Africa; UK cedes Helgoland to Germany

1890 Koninklijke Nederlandse Petroleum Maatschappij (Royal Dutch Petroleum Company) founded
1890-1898 Emma of Waldeck-Pyrmont, Queen-Regent of The Netherlands
1890-1905 Adolf, last Duke of Nassau-Welburg, Grand Duke of Luxembourg
1890-1948 Reign of Queen Wilhelmina of The Netherlands
1891 Philips brothers Frederik and Gerard found an electric light bulb factory in Eindhoven (N. Bra.)
1891 Christian Union established in Belgium

1891 Last Sioux Indians subjugated; ending the ethnic cleansing in the US, after two centuries

1893 Introduction of voting rights for males from age 25 in Belgium

1893 Voting right for women for the first time introduced in New Zealand

1892-1917 'French-Russian Alliance' Counterweight for the Triple Alliance; ends isolation of France and undermines the supremacy of the German Empire

1894 Alfred Dreyfus, Jewish-French officer, sentenced to life imprisonment for high-treason

1894 'Lombok Expedition' Revolt suppressed on the island of Lombok, Netherlands East Indies

1894-1895 'First Sino-Japanese War' Primarily over control of Korea; China cedes Taiwan, Korea becomes independent from China

1894-1917 Tsar Nicolas II reigns in Russia

1895 Revolt in Congo suppressed

1895 Guglielmo Marconi, Italian inventor, successfully completes his wireless radio system

1895-1896 'First Italo-Ethiopian War'

1895-1985 'French West Africa' Federation of the eight French coastal colonies, originally established as trading posts

1896 'Battle of Adwa' decides the First Italo-Ethiopian War in favour of Ethiopia; secures the distinction of being the first African nation to resist European colonialism

1896 Madagascar annexed by the French

1896 First modern Olympic Games in Athens; initiative of Pierre de Coubertin, French historian

1898 *Equality Law* French and Dutch languages on equal footing in Belgium

1898 Germany expands its navy to protect its colonies

1898 Russian Social Democratic Labour Party founded; operates from abroad

1898 'Spanish-American War' Spain relinquishes sovereignty over Cuba, cedes Philippine Islands, Puerto Rico and Guam to the US

1898 US annexes Hawaiian Islands

1898 Marie Curie, Polish physicist and chemist, and French husband, physicist Pierre Curie, discover the elements polonium and radium; two Nobel Prizes
1898 Émile Zola, French writer, publishes an open letter, which leads to the exoneration of the falsely accused and convicted officer Alfred Dreyfus

' J'accuse…!'
'I accuse…!', BEGINNING OF ZOLA'S OPEN LETTER

1899 'First Hague Peace Conference' initiated by Tsar Nicolas II;
Permanent Court of Arbitration for Intergovernmental Disputes established in The Hague
From 1899 The Hague develops as the international city of peace, law and security

1899 Sir Edward Elgar, English composer, completes one of his best known compositions *Enigma Variations*
1899-1901 'Boxer Rebellion' Anti-colonialist and anti-Christian movement by the Righteous Harmony Society in China versus the Eight Nation Alliance of Japan and western nations; Qing dynasty greatly weakened, indemnity imposed on China
1899-1902 'Second Anglo-Boer War' Volunteers from 12 countries assist the Transvaal and Orange Free State to no avail; British use concentration camps for whites and blacks, twenty-five thousand lives lost

1900 Queen Wilhelmina sends HNLMS Gelderland to evacuate Paul Kruger, President of the South African Republic; despite a British blockade

1900 Ferdinand, Count von Zeppelin, German aircraft manufacturer, produces the first navigable airship

1900 Marriage of Prince Albert of Belgium with Elisabeth, Duchess of Bavaria

1900 Max Planck, German physicist, awarded a Nobel Prize for the discovery of the quantum theory

From 1900 Waterworks and sewage widely installed; public health greatly improved

1901 *Ethical Policy* Strategy to make local population more independent introduced in Netherlands East Indies

1901 Queen Wilhelmina marries Prince Henry of Mecklenburg (Ger.)

'Nur einen deutschen Prinzen soll Sie bekommen'

'Only a German Prince should she have', SAID GERMAN EMPEROR WILHELM II

1901 Jacobus Henrikus van 't Hoff obtains the first Nobel Prize for The Netherlands and the first in chemistry

1901 'Commonwealth of Australia' The six colonies in Australia become a federation; first self-governing member of the British Empire

1901-1904 *Discovery Expedition* Robert Falcon Scott, Royal Navy officer and explorer, leads the expedition to Antarctica

1901-1909 Theodore Roosevelt, President of the United States of America

1901-1983 Life of Leopold III, Prince of Belgium

1902 'Treaty of Vereniging' ends hostilities of the Anglo-Boer War and the self-government of the South African Republic and Orange Free State; both Boer Republics come under sovereignty of the British Crown

1902-1912 Reign of William IV, Grand Duke of Luxembourg

1902-1923 'Anglo-Japanese Alliance' Diplomatic milestone to slow down Russian expansion in Asia; ends Britain's splendid isolation, after having not joined the Triple Alliance in 1882

1903 Wright brothers, Orville and Wilbur, American bicycle manufacturers, invent three-axis control for aircrafts; accomplish first motorised flight

1903 Russian Social Democratic Labour Party splits into Mensheviks (minority) under Julius Martov and Bolsheviks (majority) under Vladimer Lenin and Leon Trotski

1904 First Nobel Prize (for Peace) in Belgium for the Institute of International Law in Ghent (E. Fla.)

1904 'Entente Cordiale' Mutual military support between United Kingdom and the French Republic in the event of war with Germany; marks the end of a millennium of conflicts

1904 Sigmund Freud, Austrian neurologist, who founded the psychoanalytic school of psychiatry, publishes *Psychopathology of Everyday Life*

1904-1905 'Russo-Japanese War' Conflict of rival ambitions over Manchuria and Korea; Russia humiliated, contributes to the imminent Russian Revolution

1904-1908 'Herero Genocide' First genocide of the 20th century, occurs in German South West Africa (Namibia)

1906 'First Moroccan Crisis' Germany resents France's increasing dominance of Morocco; international control over police forces in the ports of Morocco

1906-1908 'Bali War' Insurrection on the island of Bali, Netherlands East Indies

1907 'Second Hague Peace Conference' Few major decisions; did enlarge the machinery for voluntary arbitration

'I have asked the Powers to join with this Government in a second Hague Conference at which it is hoped the work already so happily begun may be carried some steps further towards completion'

THEODORE ROOSEVELT

1907 'Triple Entente' Name given to alliances between France, Russia and UK, after Russia signed Anglo-Russian Entente, along with Franco-Russian Alliance and Entente Cordiale; Triple Entente and agreements with Japan, Portugal, Spain and US constitutes a counterweight to the Triple Alliance dominated by Germany

1907 Luxembourg revokes the Salic Law

1907 'Union of South Africa' unites the colonies Cape, Natal, Orange Free State and the Transvaal

1908 Heike Kamerlingh Onnes, Dutch physicist and Nobel laureate, liquefies helium for the first time
1908 Congo transferred to the State of Belgium
1909-1934 Reign of Albert I, King of the Belgians

1910 Korea annexed by Japan
1911 Roald Amundsen, Norwegian polar explorer, first man to reach the South Pole
1911 'Xingai Revolution' Uprising in Wuchang, on the Yangtze River; Sun Yat-sen, Chinese physician and revolutionary leader, forms the Chinese National People's Party Kuomintang
1911 'Second Moroccan Crisis' between Germany and France; Germany obtains swath of French Congo
1911 Chinese Emperor Puyi abdicates, Sun Yat-sen installed as President of Republic of China; annuls ancient Manchu order for men to wear pigtails
1911-1916 Sir Winston Churchill, English officer, politician and statesman, First Lord of the Admiralty; until the disaster of Gallipoli (Turk.)

1911-1942 Italy occupies the Ottoman province of Libya; third of the population dies in concentration camps

1911-1950 China permits de facto a theocratic regime under Dalai Lama in Tibet

1912 RMS Titanic strikes an iceberg and sinks on her maiden voyage

1912 France establishes a protectorate over Morocco

1912-1913 'First Balkan War' pits Balkan League (Bulgaria, Greece, Montenegro and Serbia) against Ottoman Empire; remaining European territories of Ottoman Empire apportioned

1912-1915 Yuan Shikai, Chinese general and politician, President of the Republic of China; carried out a short-lived attempt to revive a Chinese monarchy

1912-1916 China politically fragmented; warlords exercise control over their territories

1912-1919 Reign of Maria Adelheid, Grand Duchess of Luxembourg

1913 'Second Balkan War' Bulgaria dissatisfied with its share of spoils of the First Balkan War, attacks its former allies; Bulgaria defeated, gives up most of its First Balkan War gains, Serbia left as only ally of Bulgaria in the region

1913 Sir Charlie Chaplin, English comic actor and film director, produces his first silent film *The Tramp*

World Wars

1914 Archduke Franz Ferdinand, heir to the Austrian-Hungarian throne, assassinated in Sarajevo (Bosn. & Herz.)

Low Countries

1914 German troops attack and almost completely occupy Belgium and Luxembourg; The Netherlands remain neutral
1914 British Expeditionary Force sent to Belgium

1914 'Battle of the Yzer (river in W. Flan.)' Germany does not succeed in defeating the Belgian Army, contributes to establishment of the western front; leads to increased Flemish consciousness in Francophone-dominated Belgian society

1914-1918 Trench warfare in Belgium

Wider World

1914 'July Crisis' Ultimatum from Austria-Hungary to Serbia, which maintains an uncompromising position; leads through a chain of European alliances to World War I

1914 'Battle of the Falkland Islands (S. Atl. Oc.)' British fleet destroys German cruiser squadron

1914 'Battle of the Marne (river in Fr.)' results in an Allied victory against the German Army; ends the month-long German offensive
1914 Gold Standard evaporates
1914 Panama Canal opened, connects Pacific Ocean with Atlantic Ocean; President Theodore Roosevelt allows Ferdinand de Lesseps to finish the job he started
1914 UK annexes Cyprus

1914-1918 Trench warfare in France
1915 Italy, first with the Central Powers (Germany, Austria-Hungary, Ottoman Empire), joins the Allies; declares war on Austria-Hungary
1915 'Armenian Genocide' Ottoman Empire deports 1.5 million Armenians to the deserts of Syria and Iraq
1915 Albert Einstein, German-Swiss physicist, philosopher and Nobel Laureate, develops the theory of general relativity

$E=mc^2$

EINSTEIN'S EQUATION RELATING ENERGY AND MASS

1915-1916 'Gallipoli (Turk.) Campaign' Joint British and French operation to capture Ottoman capital of Istanbul and secure a route to Russia; attempt fails with heavy causalities

1916 'Battle of the Somme (river in Fr.)'pits the British and French Armies against the German Army on both banks of the river; tanks used for the first time, more than one and a half million casualties

1916 'Easter Rising' Insurrection staged in Ireland during Easter Week against British rule; succeeds in bringing physical force back into the Republican movement

1916-1918 'Arab Revolt' with success against the Ottoman Turks in the Middle East, with a liaison role for British lieutenant colonel T. E. Lawrence (of Arabia); leads to the formation of Iraq and Jordan

1916 Franz Joseph I of Austria-Hungary dies; Charles I succeeds him

1916 Grigori Rasputin, Russian mystic, killed; perceived as having influenced the latter days of the family of the Russian Tsar

1916 'Battle of Jutland (Den.)' Largest naval battle of WW I; British dominance of the North Sea maintained

1917 General male suffrage introduced in The Netherlands; women electable in national elections

1917 *Pacification of 1917* Christian and public schools obtain same subsidy in The Netherlands

1917 *Mata Hari,* Dutch exotic dancer Magaretha Zelle, accused, probably wrongly, of spying for Germany, executed by firing squad in Paris

1917 Germany declares U-boats will engage in unrestricted submarine warfare
1917 'Russian Revolution' Nicholas II abdicates; Vladimir Lenin, Russian revolutionary, assumes power as Chairman of the Council of People's Commissars
1917 US declare war on Germany and Austria-Hungary
1917 US seize Dutch merchant ships in US ports to transport US troops to France
1917 UK conquers Egypt and Jeruzalem from the Ottoman Turks
1917 Arthur Balfour, British Foreign Secretary, supports the Zionist movement with promise of a homeland in Palestine; still bone of contention for the Middle East

'His Majesty's government view with favour the establishment in Palestine of a national home for the Jewish people, and will use their best endeavours to facilitate the achievement of this object, it being clearly understood that nothing shall be done which may prejudice the civil and religious rights of existing non-Jewish communities in Palestine, or the rights and political status enjoyed by Jews in any other country.'
Arthur Balfour's letter to Walter Rothschild, leader of the Zionist Movement

1917 Erich Maria Remarque, German author, completes his anti-war novel *All Quiet on the western Front*
1917 Two Nobel Laureates, Ernest Rutherford, New Zealand chemist and physicist, who proposes a model of the atom with protons, and Sir James Chadwick, English physicist, who discovers the neutron, open the nuclear era

1917-1931 *De Stijl* Art movement of Dutch painters and designers, including Piet Mondriaan and Gerrit Rietveld

1918 'Peace of Brest-Litovsk (Belarus)' between Soviet Republic and the Central Powers; marks Russia's exit from WW I

1918 'Treaty of Sèvres (Fr.)' consolidates the partitioning of the Ottoman Empire, in accordance with secret agreements among the Allied Powers

1918 Pieter Jelles Troelstra, Dutch lawyer and socialist politician, remembered for his fight for general suffrage; fails to start a socialist revolution

1918 Queen Wilhelmina defies British blockade by letting the Dutch Navy escort a commercial fleet on its way to Netherlands East Indies

1918 Revolutionary revolts in Germany

1918 Emperor Wilhelm II of Germany abdicates and escapes to The Netherlands; armistice

'The march of the Allied Forces at the Champs Elysee in Paris lasted for three hours. With the same speed the march of the victims would have lasted eleven days and nights!'

Observes an officer, in charge of identifying dead bodies

1918 Double Monarchy Austria-Hungary dissolved; Emperor Charles I renounces participation in state affairs

1918 Compulsory school attendance up to the age of 14 in Belgium

1919 'Treaty of Versailles' Belgium obtains German speaking Eupen and Malmédy and mandate over Ruanda Urundi; demands for Dutch Flanders (Zee.) and Limburg denied

1919 'Treaty of Versailles' Austria, Hungary, Czechoslovakia and Yugoslavia separated, France obtains Lorraine, Poland obtains Posen, western Prussia and Upper Silesia, northern Schleswig-Holstein goes to Denmark, Germany obliged to disarm and pay $400 billion in reparations; increasing German resentment leads to WW II

1919 First radio transmission in The Netherlands

Low Countries

1919 Anthony Fokker, Dutch aircraft manufacturer and aviation pioneer; establishes the Netherlands Airplane Factory
1919 General women suffrage attained in The Netherlands

1919 Compulsory voting for males aged 21 and older introduced in Belgium

1919-1964 Reign of Charlotte, Grand Duchess of Luxembourg

1920 Permanent Court of International Justice established in The Hague

1921 Right to strike and 8-hour working day introduced in Belgium

Wider World

1919 'League of Nations' founded as result of the Treaty of Versailles, primary goal to prevent war; Japanese demand for equal treatment of all races denied

1919 Rosa Luxemburg, Polish-German philosopher and Marxist activist, murdered
1919-1921 'Irish War of Independence' Guerrilla war mounted by the Irish Republican Army (IRA) against the British government
1919-1933 'Weimar Republic' Parliamentary republic replaces the imperial form of government in Germany

1920 US Senate rejects again the Treaty of Versailles; 'Knox-Poster Resolution' ends US involvement in WW I in 1921
1920 'National Socialist German Workers' Party' (NSDAP) founded; Adolf Hitler, German corporal from Bohemia (Czech.), becomes its Führer
1920 US do not become member of the League of Nations; Russia is not admitted

1920 'Kapp-putsch' Coup attempt to overthrow the Weimar Republic in Germany fails
1920-1933 *Prohibition* Period during which sale, manufacture and transportation of alcohol is banned in the US; many social problems attributed to alcohol

1921 Economic agreement between Belgium and Luxembourg

1922 Women are allowed to vote for the first time in The Netherlands

1921 'Mandate of Mesopotamia (Iraq)' entrusted to the UK by the League of Nations; poison gas used against revolting Shia and Sunni Arabs
1921 'Anglo-Irish Treaty' concludes Irish War of Independence; establishes Irish Free State as a dominion, Northern Ireland opted out

1922 'March on Rome' Fascists march to Rome under Benito Mussolini, Italian journalist, who becomes Prime Minister
1922 'Treaty of Rapallo (It.)' Weimar Republic is the first country to recognise Soviet Union; treaty renounces Russian territorial and financial claims from WW I
1922-1923 'Irish Civil War' rages between two opposing groups of Irish nationalists; won by the Free State Forces
1923 Kuomintang Army led by General Chiang Kai-shek conquers southern China
1923 Gustav Stresemann, German Liberal politician and statesman, Chancellor of Germany during the Weimar Republic; supports democracy and envisages European economic integration
1923 French and Belgian forces occupy the Ruhrgebiet (Ger.), as reprisal after Germany failed to fulfil reparation payments as demanded by the Versailles Treaty; leads to hyperinflation in Germany
1923 Adolf Hitler in prison after participation in a failed coup; writes *Mein Kampf* (My Struggle)
1923-1938 Mustafa Kemal (Perfection) Atatürk, Turkish General and President of the Republic of Turkey; transforms the former Ottoman Empire into a modern and secular nation-state

1924 Lenin dies; Joseph Stalin, Soviet politician from Georgia, becomes leader of the Soviet Union, rules as dictator
1924-1943 Fascist dictatorship in Italy under Mussolini (Il Duce), after winning the elections
1924-1994 *Apartheid* Racial separation in the South African Republic practised
1925 Sun Yat-sen dies; Chiang Kai-shek succeeds him as leader of the Kuomintang
1925 Britain returns to the Gold Standard

1925-1926 Hendrikus Colijn, Dutch politician, Prime Minister and Minister of Finance

1925-1941 Reign of Reza Shah, Persian Cossack general, Shah of Imperial Iran

1926 Belgium adopts the Gold Standard

1926 'Treaty of Locarno (Swit.)' WW I Allied powers leave borders in central and eastern Europe open for revision, but guarantee the borders in western Europe; Allied troops withdraw from Rhineland (German territory west of the Rhine), normalises relations with Germany
1926 Germany member of the League of Nations
1926-1935 Józef Pilsudski, Marshal and leader of the Second Polish Republic; founder of the modern Polish state

'Every honest Pole spits when he hears the word Locarno!'
PILSUDSKI

1926 John Logie Baird, Scottish engineer, invents the first practical television system

1926 Leopold, Prince of Belgium, marries Astrid Thyra, Princess of Sweden
1927 Address by King Albert I in Seraing (Lièg.)

'There is a real crisis of the scientific and research institutions in Belgium'
ALBERT I

1928 D.H. Lawrence, English author, poet and playwright, publishes his famous novel *Lady Chatterley's Lover*

1928 Summer Olympics in Amsterdam; Olympic flame re-introduced

1928 After seizing Beijing, Chiang Kai-shek leads the national government of China from the former southern capital of Nanking

1928 Sir Alexander Fleming, Scottish biologist and pharmacologist, discovers penicillin

1929 *Wall Street Crash* Stock market crash in US; 10-year economic slump affects western industrial countries

'It's only when the tide goes out that one can see who is swimming naked'
Warren Buffett, born 1930, looking back in history

1929 Ernest Hemingway, American author and Nobel Prize Laureate, completes his novel *A Farewell to Arms*

1930 Economic crisis and inflation in Germany; nazis and communists gain in elections

1930 *Smoot-Hawley Tariff Act* introduced in the US; import duty of 40% paralyses world trade

1930 *Salt March* Mahatma Gandhi leads non-violent protest against the British salt tax in colonial India; round-table conference between Viceroy Lord Irwin and Gandhi convened

'There is no people on earth who would not prefer their own bad government to good government from an alien power'
Gandhi to Lord Irwin

1930 University of Ghent (E. Flan.) adopts Dutch as its official language
1931 One official language only in Flanders and in Wallonia; separate arrangements for Brussels
1931 Anton Mussert, Dutch engineer, founds the National Socialist Movement (NSB) in The Netherlands

1931 'Statute of Westminster' establishes equality for self-governing dominions of the British Empire and UK, with the exception of India
1932 UK recognises independence of the Kingdom of Saudi-Arabia
1932 'Mukden Incident' Under a pretext the Japanese Army invades Manchuria; establishes the Manchuria State with Puyi, the last Qing Emperor of China, as Emperor

1932 'Treaty of Ouchy (Swit.)' Benelux countries lower their import duties; discontent in UK and US
1932 Zuiderzee (bay of the North Sea) closed; following a plan of Cornelis Lely, Dutch engineer and minister

'A people that lives, works for its future'
EMBLAZONED ON THE MONUMENT MARKING THE POINT OF CLOSURE OF THE LONGEST DAM ON EARTH

1933 Mutiny on board HNLMS De Zeven Provinciën, plying Netherlands East Indies waters
1933 NSB uniforms forbidden in The Netherlands

1933 Nazis win elections, Adolf Hitler appointed Chancellor; Germany's membership of League of Nations cancelled
1933 Gold Standard abandoned almost everywhere

1933-1939 Hendrikus Colijn, Prime Minister of five consecutive cabinets in The Netherlands

1934 'Jordaan Riot' to increase unemployment benefits in Amsterdam

1934 Marinus van der Lubbe, Dutch communist, beheaded after controversially being accused of setting the German Reichstag Building in Berlin on fire

1934-1951 Reign of Leopold III, King of the Belgians
1935 Astrid, Queen of the Belgians, dies in a car accident with Leopold III at the wheel
1935 NSB obtains 8% of the vote in elections for the Provincial States of The Netherlands

1933-1936 *New Deal* Economic programmes to respond to the Great Depression implemented
1933-1945 Franklin D. Roosevelt, President of the United States of America

1934 'Long March' Mao Zedong, Chinese politician and statesman, leads retreat by the Red Army of the Chinese Communist Party to evade pursuit by Kuomintang; travels over 8000 miles to the province of Shaanxi (N. China)

1934-1938 'Great Purge' Joseph Stalin purges the party and the army; millions of deaths in Russia

1935 Sir Robert Watson-Watt, Scottish engineer, inventor of radar; provides vital advance information which helps to win the Air Battle of Britain in WW II
1935 Germany re-arms and re-introduces compulsory conscription; violation of the Versailles Treaty
1935 'Second Italo-Ethiopian War' Occupation of Ethiopian Empire and annexation as colony of Italian East Africa; Emperor Haile Selassie I in exile

1936 Adolf Hitler renounces the Treaty of Locarno and occupies the Rhineland

'Although the chance of neutrality looks considerably smaller than in 1914, you can sleep peacefully'
PRIME MINISTER COLIJN OF THE NETHERLANDS, RADIO TRANSMISSION, 1936

1936 John Maynard Keynes, English economist, influences the theory of macroeconomics as well as the economic policy of governments with his book *The General Theory of Employment, Interest and Money*

'In the long run we are all dead, but there will always be taxes!'
KEYNES

1936 University of Leuven (Fl. Bra.) becomes bi-lingual (Dutch and French)

1936 Pablo Picasso, Spanish painter and sculptor, paints his famous work *Guernica*; portrayal of German bombing of this city during the Spanish Civil War
1936-1939 'Spanish Civil War' begins with a coup d'état by generals, supported by nationalists (helped by Hitler and Mussolini), cconservatives, fascists and monarchists under Generalissimo Francisco Franco against republicans, communists (helped by Stalin), anarchists and international volunteers; both sides test modern weapons
1936-1947 Francisco Franco (Caudillo, leader) head of the Spanish State; becomes a dictator

1937 Princess Juliana marries Bernhard, Prince of Lippe-Biesterveld
1937 NSB obtains 4 % of the votes in the election for the Parliament in The Netherlands

1937 Sir Frank Whittle, British Royal Air Force (RAF) engineer officer, hailed as the father of jet propulsion

1937 *Hindenburg Disaster* Hydrogen-filled Zeppelin catches fire, while docking at its mooring mast at Lakehurst, NY; marks the end of the airship era

1937 Irish Free State comes to an end, succeeded by the sovereign State of Ireland

1937-1945 'Second Sino-Japanese War' Japan attacks China from Manchuria and cruelly occupies Beijing, Shanghai and Nanking; after the Japanese attack on Pearl Harbour (1942) the war merges into WW II and accounts for more than half of the casualties in the Pacific area

1938 Beatrix, Princess of Orange-Nassau born

1938 'Anschluss' Stage-managed occupation and annexation of Austria by Germany

1938 Neville Chamberlain, Prime Minister of the UK, visits Adolf Hitler in Munich (Ger.)

'I believe it is peace for our time'
CHAMBERLAIN ON HIS RETURN TO LONDON

1938 Germany occupies first Sudetenland (West Czechoslovakia), then the rest of Czechoslovakia

1939 'Molotov-Ribbentrop Pact' Germany and Russia pledge to remain neutral in the event either nation were to be attacked by a third party; secret protocol divides northern and eastern Europe into German and Soviet spheres of influence

1939 Germany occupies western Poland, Russia occupies eastern Poland, Britain and France declare war on Germany; leads to WW II, the largest military conflict ever, claiming fifty million lives

1939-1940 Winston Churchill appointed First Lord of the Admiralty of the UK
1939-1940 'Winter War' Soviet offensive against Finland, ends after heavy Russian losses, with 'Moscow Peace Treaty'; part of Finland ceded to Russia, Finland's independence preserved
1940 'Katyn Massacre' Soviet Politburo, including Joseph Stalin, orders the mass murder of twenty-two thousand Polish officers, officials, priests and doctors in the woods near Katyn (Rus.)
1940 Germany invades Denmark, France and Norway

1940 Germany occupies Belgium, The Netherlands and Luxembourg; Rotterdam subjected to terror-bombing by the Luftwaffe
1940 Queen Wilhelmina and the Dutch government leave and reside in London until 1945

'The only man in the Dutch government is a woman'
SIR WINSTON CHURCHILL

1940 Winston Churchill, Prime Minister of the UK

'I have nothing to offer but blood, toil, tears and sweat'
SIR WINSTON CHURCHILL

1940 'Miracle of Dunkirk' Three hundred and fifty thousand Allied soldiers rescued from the beaches near Dunkirk (Fr.) and brought to the UK, partly by private boats
1940 Capitulation of France; French Marshal Philippe Pétain collaborates with the Germans as President of Vichy France in southern France

1940 Charles de Gaulle, French general and statesman, unites and leads the Free French Forces outside France during WW II

1940 Leon Trotski murdered in Mexico

1940 Palaeolithic cave paintings discovered in Lascaux (Fr.); seventeen thousand years old

1940 Japan joins Germany and Italy in WW II

1940 Comedy film *The Great Dictator* written and directed by its star actor Charlie Chaplin; bitterly satirises Adolf Hitler

1940-1941 'Battle of Britain' Air campaign waged by the German Air Force against the UK to gain air superiority over the RAF; decisive British victory, first turning point in the WW II

1940-1944 Leopold III remains as prisoner of war in Laken (Brussels); tries to run a semi-independent government, disapproved by the Belgian government in London

1940-1944 Marshal Pétain governs Vichy France

1940-1945 'Enigma Machine' in use by the Axis (German and Japanese) Armies for encryption of messages; the Allied Forces break the code which hasten the end of WW II by an estimated two years

1941 'February Strike' National protest against German round-ups of Jews in The Netherlands

1941 'Pearl Harbor' Surprise strike by Japan on the US naval base at Pearl Harbor (Hawaii); next day the US declare war on Japan

1941 British Army conquers Ethiopia; Emperor Haile Selassie I returns to his throne

1941 *Soldier of Orange*, Siebern Erik Hazelhoff Roelfzema, Dutch agent and wartime RAF pilot, makes his crossing to England

1941 'Operation Barbarossa' Germany invades Russia; Red Army repels the Wehrmacht's advances, but Russia's situation remains dire

1941 In Germany and in the German-occupied areas all Jews over the age of 6 are required to wear the yellow Star of David

1941 Iran occupied by the Allied Forces to secure their oil interests; Shah Khan Reza banished

1941-1979 Mohammad Reza Pahlavi, son of Khan Reza, reigns as Shah of Persia; acts as a despot

1941 King Leopold III marries Lilian Baels, daughter of a ship-owner and politician from Ostend (W. Flan.); becomes Princess of Réthy

1942 Japan declares war on The Netherlands, invades Netherlands East Indies

1942 Singapore and Malaysia surrender to Japanese forces

1942 'Battle of the Java Sea (Netherlands East Indies)' Dutch Lieutenant-Admiral Conrad Helfrich, commander of a combined Allied fleet, sends Karel Doorman, Dutch Rear Admiral, and the major part of the fleet, with no air support or radio communication, on unsuccessful mission to fight the Japanese invasion fleet

'To All Ships, I Attack, Follow Me.'

Karel Doorman's flagsignal, just before he dies

1942 'Wannsee Conference' plans the final solution to the Jewish question, by deportation of the entire Jewish population to eastern Europe; results in the 'Holocaust' with six million deaths
1942 'Battle of El Alamein (Egyp.)' Bernard Montgomery (Monty), British Field Marshal, defeats German Field Marshal Erwin Rommel; ends Axis' hopes of control of the Suez Canal and access to the Middle Eastern oil fields, second turning point of WW II

1942-1944 Dutch diarist Anne Frank hides in a secret annexe to a building in Amsterdam; dies in 1945 in Bergen Belsen (Ger.)
1942-1945 Netherlands East Indies occupied by Japan; Dutch civilians and soldiers held in concentration camps

1942-1945 'The Fourth Ally' Netherlands forces escape from Netherlands East Indies to Australia; actively support the American, Australian and British forces during the ensuing Pacific War, Dutch merchant vessels make a substantial contribution
1943 'Casablanca Conference' Churchill, De Gaulle and Roosevelt plan their European war strategy
1943 Germans surrender in northern Africa and near Stalingrad (Rus.)
1943 'Warsaw Ghetto Uprising' Jewish resistance in German-occupied Warsaw, opposes Nazi transports of Jews to concentration camps
1943 'Tank Battle of Kursk (Rus.)' Largest armoured clash ends in a decisive Soviet victory; third turning point of WW II, a war which costs Russia in total thirty million lives
1943 Albert Hofmann, Swiss scientist, synthesises the psychedelic LSD

1943 'Invasion of Sicily (It.)' Allies take Sicily in an amphibious and airborne operation against the Axis; stepping stone for the ensuing Italian Campaign

1943 Benito Mussolini toppled from power, new government of Italy breaks with Germany; however, German Army continues to occupy and fight for Italy's soil

1943 'Tehran (Iran) Conference' Churchill, Roosevelt and Stalin plan the final strategy for WW II, centred on opening a second front in western Europe

1943-1945 'Burma Railway' Hundred thousand Allied prisoners of war and Asian labourers die working on a Japanese railway between Bangkok (Thai.) and Rangoon (Myan.)

1943-1948 Chiang Kai-shek, Chairman of the Nationalist Government of China

1944 'D-Day' Hundred and fifty thousand Allied troops land on the beaches of Normandy (Fr.) in the largest amphibious operation in history; liberate France and weaken the Nazi hold on the rest of western Europe

1944 Belgian Piron Brigade and the Dutch Princess Irene Brigade participate in the liberation of Europe

1944 Claus von Stauffenberg, German Army officer and aristocrat, unsuccessfully attempts to kill Adolf Hitler; shot dead

1944 'United Nations Monetary and Financial Conference' begins at Bretton Woods, New Hamp. (US); leads to International Monetary Fund (IMF), General Agreement on Tariffs and Trade (GATT) and the World Bank

1944 'Warsaw Uprising' Attempt by the Polish Resistance to liberate Warsaw from Nazi Germany ahead of the Russian Army; Red Army stops short of Warsaw for 63 days, until the Polish Resistance surrenders to the Germans

1944 'Battle of Imphal (India)' Japanese Army attempts to invade India, but driven back by Allied forces into Burma (now Myanmar); biggest Japanese defeat on land

1944 As reprisal for an attack on one German officer, 600 men from the municipality of Putten (Gel.) die in a concentration camp

1944 Romania and Bulgaria withdraw from the war against the Soviet Union, joining the Allies; German troops leave Greece
1944 Allied troops liberate Paris

1944 Allied troops liberate Brussels and Antwerp
1944 Belgian government returns; pre-war parliament appoints government of national unity and Prince Charles, Count of Flanders, as Regent
1944 Benelux Custom Union established
1944 'Operation Market Garden' Largest Allied airborne operation of all time aims at seizure of the bridges across the Meuse and the Rhine near Arnhem (Gel.) to encircle the Ruhrgebiet; ends in an Allied withdrawal
1944 'Ardennes Offensive' Final German effort in the forested mountains of the Ardennes region (Wal. Lux.) to split the Allied Armies; results in an Allied victory
1944-1945 'Dutch Famine' in the still occupied western part of The Netherlands; twenty thousand people die

1945 'Yalta (Ukr.) Conference' Churchill, Roosevelt and Stalin discuss post-war reorganisation of Germany and the borders of Poland

1945 Leopold III liberated by US troops; rejects any reconciliation with the Belgian government

1945 US Army conquers the islands Iwo Jima and Okinawa (Jap.); bloodiest battle of the Pacific War
1945 'Arab League' established by Egypt, Iraq, Jordan, Lebanon, Saudi Arabia, Syria and Yemen in Cairo (Egyp.)
1945 Germany capitulates unconditionally
1945 'Potsdam (Ger.) Conference' Churchill (initially, later Attlee), Stalin and Truman meet to impose punishment on defeated Germany
1945 Atomic bombs dropped on Hiroshima and Nagasaki (Jap.); Japan capitulates

'Their name liveth for ever more'
UNIFORM EPITAPH, COMMONWEALTH WAR GRAVE COMMISSION

1945 United Nations (UN) established in San Francisco, Cal. (US)
1945 Korea independent from Japan, UN forms trusteeship for Korea; Soviet Union administers the peninsula north of the 38th parallel, US the southern part
1945-1953 Harry S. Truman President of the United States of America, after the demise of Franklin D. Roosevelt

After the World Wars

1945 Sukarno and Hatta, Indonesian advocates of liberty, declare Indonesia independent

1945 Winston Churchill concludes that there is an *Iron Curtain* between Russia and the West
1945-1951 Clement Attlee succeeds Winston Churchill as Prime Minister of Great Britain after a landslide election victory; first Labour Prime Minister to serve a full Parliamentary term

Low Countries

1945-1946 'Bersiap (get ready) Period' Violent and chaotic phase of Indonesia's revolutionary period at the end of WW II; activists fill the vacuum in Netherlands East Indies after the Japanese capitulation

1947 Willem Drees, then Minister of Social Affairs, introduces emergency legislation for the elderly; his name immortalised in the expression *Getting (money) from Drees*

1947-1948 The Netherlands carry out police actions in Netherlands East Indies to suppress the independence movement; however to no avail
1947-1948 Queen Wilhelmina cedes the throne temporally to her daughter Princess Juliana, who acts as Regent

Wider World

1945-1953 Last period of Stalinism; large-scale purges result in millions of deaths
1945-1969 Ho Chi Minh, Marxist revolutionary leader, President of the Democratic Republic of Vietnam

1946 The Philippines attains its independence
1947 American plane flies faster than the speed of sound for the first time

1947 'Partition of India' Muslim majority gains independence from the UK and adopts the name of Pakistan, Hindu majority gains independence from the UK and adopts the name of India

1947-1955 *Marshall Plan* Programme of the US for rebuilding and creating a stronger economy in western Europe; leads to economic recovery, also in Germany
1947-1975 Francisco Franco, Regent of the nominally restored Kingdom of Spain
1948 Burma becomes an independent republic
1948 GATT Conference in Geneva; twenty-three countries reach agreement to lower import duties

1948 Mahatma Gandhi murdered in Dehli (India)

1948 'Arab-Israeli War' Israel declares its independence, attacked by Egypt, Iraq, Jordan, Lebanon and Syria; Palestinians escape to Lebanon, Jordan and the Gaza strip

1948 Communist Party seizes control of Czechoslovakia

1948 General female suffrage in Belgium

1948 European Congress in The Hague; Council of Europe formed

1948 First television broadcast in The Netherlands

1948-1949 'Berlin Blockade' Soviet Union blocks western Allies' rail and road access to Berlin; Allies organise Berlin Airlift to carry in supplies

1948-1949 Chiang Kai-shek President of the Republic of China

1948-1951 *CoBrA* International art movement of painters and writers from **Co**penhagen, **Br**ussels and **A**msterdam

1948-1958 Willem Drees, Dutch Socialist and politician, Prime Minister in four consecutive cabinets

1948-1980 Reign of Juliana, Queen of The Netherlands

1949 Ireland formally becomes the Republic of Ireland

1949 Bundesrepublik Deutschland (BRD) (Federal Republic of Germany) established from the American, British and French occupation zones

1949 George Orwell, English author, renowned for intelligence and wit, who wrote earlier the satirical novel *Animal Farm*, completes the dystopian novel *Nineteen Eighty-Four*

'Big Brother is watching you'
GEORGE ORWELL

1949 North Atlantic Treaty Organization (NATO) established by West European states and the US; headquartered in Brussels
1949 Soviet Russia has the atomic bomb at its disposal
1949 Mao Zedong proclaims the People's Republic of China
1949 Deutsche Demokratische Republik (DDR) (German Democratic Republic) established from the Soviet occupation zone
1949 Shanghai under control of the Communist Party of China
1949 Chiang Kai-shek flees to Taiwan; continues the Republic of China there

1949 Queen Juliana grants Indonesia sovereignty; Sukarno first President of Indonesia
1949-1958 The Netherlands enjoys rapid economic recovery under Prime Minister Drees

1950 Chinese Army invades Tibet, re-establishing China's sovereignty and granting the area autonomy

1950 Referendum on return of Leopold III to the throne; profound discord in Belgium
1950 Leopold III decides to withdraw in favour of his 20-year old son Prince Boudewijn
1950 Julien Lahaut, Chairman of the Communist Party of Belgium, shouts '*Vive la République*', while Boudewijn pledges his commitment as future King; Julien Lahaut murdered shortly thereafter
1950-1951 Prince Charles acts again as Regent of Belgium

1950-1953 'Korean War' between North Korea and China with air support of Russia, and South Korea, supported by the UN; demilitarised zone established along the 38th parallel
1950-1970 Japan develops into the second largest economic power of the world

1951 Leopold III signs his abdication

'I beseech you, remain united'
LEOPOLD III

1951 'European Coal and Steel Community (ECSC)': First supranational organisation to unify western Europe established by Belgium, France, Italy, Luxembourg, The Netherlands and West Germany (BRD) under the Treaty of Paris; lays the foundation for the European Union

1951 Mohammed Mossadegh, Iranian Prime Minister, nationalises the Anglo-Persian Oil Company

1951-1993 Reign of Boudewijn I, King of the Belgians

1951-1955 Winston Churchill again Prime Minister of the UK

1953 'North Sea Flood' kills 2000 people in The Netherlands, UK and at sea; Delta Plan developed to provide future protection for The Netherlands

'Luctor et emergo'
'*I struggle and emerge*', MOTTO OF THE PROVINCE OF ZEELAND

1953 Joseph Stalin dies; Nikita Khrushchev succeeds him as leader of the Soviet Union

1953 Mohammed Mossadegh diposed; by interference of the Central Intelligence Agency (CIA) of the US

1953 Revolt in East Berlin violently suppressed

1953 Francis Crick, English molecular biologist, and James Watson, American molecular biologist, discover the molecular structure of DNA; jointly awarded the Nobel Prize with Maurice Wilkens, New Zealand-born molecular biologist

1953-1961 Under President Dwight D. Eisenhower (Ike) the US enjoy a period of economic growth

1954 'Battle of Dien Bien Phu (Viet.)' French Expeditionary Corps defeated by Viet Minh communists; Vietnam becomes independent, but splits up into a northern and southern part, Laos and Cambodia also independent from France

'The last time the Chinese came here, they stayed a thousand years.
The French are foreigners.
They are weak. Colonialism is dying. The white man is finished in Asia.'
Ho Chi Minh

1954 Statute for the Kingdom of The Netherlands in force; Surinam and the Netherlands Antilles obtain – within the Kingdom – their own government and legal powers

From 1954 Political party Volksunie carries Flemish nationalism into the Belgian political arena

1955 'Warsaw Pact' Mutual defence treaty by eight communist states in eastern Europe at Russia's initiative; counter force to NATO

1955 West Germany (BRD) becomes member of NATO; allowed to re-arm

1955 'Austrian Independence Treaty' signed between the Allied occupying powers and the Austrian government; re-establishes Austria as a sovereign state

1956 'Suez Crisis' War fought by Britain, France and Israel against Egypt, following Egypt's decision to nationalise the Suez Canal; Anglo-French withdrawal, Israel occupies the Sinai desert

1956 Malcom McLean, American entrepreneur, develops sea container; changes the traditional way of loading and discharging cargo onto ships and lorries

1956 Khrushchev's speech *On the Personality Cult and its Consequences* denounces Stalin's dictatorial rule; leads to revolts in Poland and Hungary

Low Countries

1956 Algemene Ouderdoms Wet (AOW) (State Pension Law) established in The Netherlands; continuation of the temporary law from 1947

1958 Benelux Economic Union comes into force; strengthens the bonds between Belgium, Luxembourg and The Netherlands

1958 *School Pact* ends the struggle about financing schools in Belgium

1958 *Expo'58* First World Exhibition after WW II, in Brussels; symbol *Atomium*

Wider World

1957 Launch of the first earth-orbiting satellite *Sputnik* by the Soviet Union; ushers in political, military and scientific developments, start of the space age

1957 Ghana independent from Britain

1957 'Little Rock (Ark. US) Crisis' African-American students prevented from entering a segregated school; resolved after intervention of President Eisenhower

1957 'Treaty of Rome' European Economic Community (EEC) established by Belgium, France, Italy, Luxembourg, The Netherlands and West Germany (BRD); second international organisation based on supranationalism, after the ECSC

1958 Plebiscite for independence of Algeria results in a landslide victory; leads to political crisis in France

'Je vous ai compris'

'I have understood you', shouted De Gaulle, in front of a crowd of Pied-Noirs, French colonists in Algeria

Low Countries

From 1958 Brussels develops into the 'Capital' of the European Union

1959 Large gas field discovered in Slochteren (Gro.)

Wider World

1959-1969 De Gaulle supervises the writing of a new constitution; Fifth Republic founded and De Gaulle elected President

Low Countries

Wider World

1960 Belgian Congo becomes independent as Republic of the Congo

1960 Nigeria gains its independence from the UK

From 1960 Moroccans, Turks and refugees from war areas move to western Europe

1960-1980 *Asian Tigers* such as Korea, Malaysia, Singapore and Taiwan follow Japan's example and adopt western economic growth factors

1961 Patrick Lumumba, Prime Minister of Congo, murdered

1961 'Berlin Wall' cuts off West Berlin from surrounding East Germany and East Berlin; symbolises the Iron Curtain between western and eastern Europe

1961-1963 John F. Kennedy, President of the United States of America

1962 'Cuban Missile Crisis' Soviet and Cuban governments start to build bases for ballistic nuclear missiles in Cuba, following the deployment of US missiles in Italy and Turkey; almost leads to a third World War, Moscow-Washington hot line installed

1962 Queen Wilhelmina dies

'Lonely, but not alone'

Title of Wilhelmina's autobiography

1962 'Treaty of New York' transfers Netherlands New Guinea to Indonesia

1962 Algeria independent from France

1962 Belgium's mandate over Urundi and Rwanda (Rwanda and Burundi) ends

1962 Language boundaries established in Belgium; areas delineated in accordance with the territorial principle

1962-1975 Many British and French colonies in Africa become independent

'Ich bin ein Berliner'

Kennedy, visiting the Berlin Wall in 1963

1963 President John F. Kennedy murdered in Dallas, Texas (US)

1963 Martin Luther King Jr., American clergyman, leader of the African-American civil rights movement, leads the *March on Washington*

'I had a dream ...'
MARTIN LUTHER KING JR.

1963-1969 Lyndon B. Johnson, President of the United States of America

1964 *Civil Rights Act* outlaws discrimination against African-Americans and women; ends racial segregation in schools

1964 'Gulf of Tonkin Incident' Sea battle between one US destroyer and three North Vietnamese torpedo boats; serves to justify start of open US warfare against North Vietnam

1964-1966 *Provo* (non-violent anarchism) causes an era of communal unrest in The Netherlands

1964-1982 Leonid Brezhnev replaces Nikita Khrushchev as General Secretary of the Communist Party; beginning of economic stagnation, which leads to the dissolution of the Soviet Union

1964-2000 Reign of Jean, Grand Duke of Luxembourg

1965 'Indo-Pakistani War' Skirmishes over the region of Kashmir lying between the two countries

1965-1979 Rhodesia declares itself independent from the UK

1966 Princess Beatrix marries Claus von Amsberg, Prince of The Netherlands

1966-1976 'Cultural Revolution' Violent social, political and economic mass upheavals in China; ends with Mao Zedong's death, the arrest of the 'Gang of Four' and millions of deaths

1967 Crown Prince William-Alexander of Orange-Nassau born

1967 'Six Day War' fought between Israel and Egypt, Jordan, Syria and Arab Expeditionary Forces; Israel seizes from its opponents Gaza Strip, Sinai Peninsula, West Bank, East Jerusalem and Golan Heights, occupied territories and refugee problems have global consequences
1967 'ASEAN' South East Asian organisation established by Indonesia, Malaysia, Philippines Singapore and Thailand; cooperates with China, Japan and South Korea
1968 *May 1968* General strike brings the French economy to a virtual standstill; almost causes the collapse of De Gaulle's government
1968 Martin Luther King Jr. murdered in Memphis, Tennessee (US)
1968 'Prague Spring' Russian invasion of Czechoslovakia
1968 'Non-proliferation Treaty' originally ratified by the nuclear states Russia, UK and US in 1968, and later by China and France in 1992; to limit the spread of nuclear weapons

1969 Oil and natural gas in reservoirs discovered beneath the North Sea

1969 Neil Armstrong, American astronaut; first man on the moon

'That's one small step for man; one giant leap for mankind'
NEIL ARMSTRONG, JUST BEFORE STEPPING ONTO THE MOON

1969-1974 Richard Nixon, President of the United States of America
1970 Richard Nixon begins withdrawal of US Army from Vietnam

1970 'First State Reform' Belgium becomes a federal state, with Flemish, Walloon and Brussels regions with equal representation in the Council of Ministers; Dutch, French and German Cultural Communities established
1970-1972 French-speaking Roman Catholic University established in Louvain-le-Neuve (Wal. Bra.); splits off from the Dutch-speaking Catholic University of Leuven (Fl. Bra.)

1971 'Bangladesh Liberation War' pits East Pakistan and India against West Pakistan; secession of East Pakistan, which becomes independent Bangladesh
1972 Richard Nixon visits China and has talks with Mao Zedong; draws China out of its isolation
1972 People's Republic of China replaces Taiwan in the Security Council of the UN
1973 De Gaulle resigns, after losing a nationwide referendum on state reform

1973 German-speaking community in Belgium becomes self-governing within the Walloon region

1973 Denmark, Ireland and UK become members of the EEC
1973 'Yom Kippur War' Egypt and Syria attack Israel on the holiest day in Judaism; oil crisis in the western world
1974 *Watergate Scandal* results from break-in at the Democratic National Committee headquarters in Washington, DC; leads to the resignation of President Richard Nixon, the first and only resignation of any US President; Vice President Gerald Ford takes over the Presidency
1975 Spanish head of State Francisco Franco dies; King Juan Carlos I sworn in, parliamentary monarchy restored

1975 Surinam independent; a large part of its population emigrates to The Netherlands

1975 *Lockheed Bribery Scandals* A series of bribes by US aerospace company Lockheed; in The Netherlands Prince Bernhard receives $ 1.5 million, and is later stripped off the title of Inspector-General of the Army

1975 'Carnation Revolution' Portugal changes from dictatorship to democracy, after two years of social turmoil and power disputes

1975 US Army driven out of South Vietnam; the whole of Vietnam in the hands of communist Vietcong

1975-1978 Pol Pot, Cambodian dictator and leader of the Khmer Rouge, drives the entire population from the cities to the farm lands; nearly two million people are killed

1977 Deng Xiaoping, Chinese statesman, introduces economic reforms, while maintaining political structure; China rises in stature, prosperity and influence, results in enormous growth

'It does not matter if a cat is black or white, as long as it catches mice'
DENG XIAOPING

1977-1981 Jimmy Carter, President of the United States of America

1979 Ruhollah Khomeini, Iranian religious leader of the Iranian Revolution, succeeds in overthrowing Shah Mohammed Reza Pahlavi and establishes the Iranian Republic; becomes country's Supreme Leader

1979 'Egypt-Israel Peace Treaty' Egypt recognises the State of Israel; Sinai returned to Egypt

1979-1989 'Soviet War in Afghanistan' Soviet Union supports Marxist-Leninist government of Afghanistan against Mujahideen resistance supported by US, UK and Muslim nations
1979-1990 Margaret Thatcher (Iron Lady), Prime Minister of UK and leader of the Conservative Party; only woman to hold either post

1980 Princess Beatrix of Orange-Nassau crowned Queen of The Netherlands

1980 Zimbabwe is formed from the British crown colony of southern Rhodesia; Robert Mugabe elected as Prime Minister

1980 'Second State Reform' Cultural communities in Belgium become Flemish, French and German Communities for cultural, health and youth matters, Flemish Region (including Dutch-speaking inhabitants of Brussels) and Walloon Region (including French-speaking inhabitants of Brussels) with own governments established; Flanders merges its Community and Regional institutions

1980-1981 NATO installs nuclear cruise missiles in answer to Russia's continental missiles; leads to peace demonstrations throughout Europe
1980-1988 'Iran-Iraq War' Strategically and tactically an Iraqi failure, tactically an Iranian failure; UN resolution ends hostilities which include the use of poison gas by Iraq and deployment of child martyrs by Iran, one million deaths
1981 Greece becomes member of the EEC
1981-1989 Ronald Reagan, President of the United States of America
1982 'Falklands War' between Argentina and UK over the disputed Falkland Islands (S. Atl. Oc.); status quo maintained, Argentine military Junta collapses

1984 Indira Gandhi, Prime Minister of India, murdered in New Delhi
1985-1991 Michail Gorbatsjov, Party Leader and first President of the Soviet Union, eases tension between East and West

'Perestrojka, Glasnost'

'Restructuring, Openness', key words of Gorbatsjov

1986 Portugal and Spain become members of the EEC

1986 Aruba secedes from The Netherlands Antilles; becomes a country of the Kingdom of The Netherlands

1986 US bombing attack on Tripoli and Benghazi (Lib.) for supposed Libyan state-sponsored terrorism
1986 'Chernobyl Disaster' Nuclear accident at the Chernobyl nuclear power plant in Ukraine; worst nuclear power plant accident in history
1986 'Treaty of Amsterdam' emphasises citizenship and rights of individuals; Schengen Agreement (Free movement of people within the EEC) incorporated into European Law
1986 Voting power for non-EEC citizens in municipal councils

1988 'Third State Reform' Brussels-Capital Region established with its own institutions, French and Dutch speakers equally protected; legal powers of the Regions expanded with responsibility for education

1989 Soviet-Union withdraws from Afghanistan, leaving two and a half million dead; civil war breaks out
1989 Lech Walesa, Polish politician, founds the Polish non-communist trade union Solidarity at Gdansk Shipyard; elections result in a Solidarity government with Walesa as President

1989 'Tiananmen Square Massacre' Demonstrations by intellectuals result in the killing of five hundred people, during a year when a number of communist governments around the world collapse; remains forbidden topic in China
1989 Berlin Wall falls; breakdown of communism in eastern Europe
1989-1993 George Bush (Sr.), President of the United States of America
1990 Germany reunifies; incorporation of the former DDR into the Federal Republic of Germany (BRD)
From 1990 China marginalises minorities by stimulating migration of Han Chinese from China proper into Tibet and into the Uygur's province of Xinjiang
1990-1991 'Persian Gulf War' waged by UN coalition forces against Iraq, which had invaded Kuwait
1991 Soviet-Union breaks up into fifteen independent republics, of which the Russian Federation is the largest
1991 Sir Tim Berners-Lee, English computer scientist, together with Robert Cailliau, Belgian engineer, credited with inventing the World Wide Web
1991-1999 Boris Jeltsin, first President of the Russian Federation; initiates the State Duma, lower house of Russian parliament, in 1993
1992 'Treaty of Maastricht' Twelve countries of the EEC become the European Union (EU); creation of a single European currency, the euro

1993 Boudewijn I dies; his brother succeeds him as Albert II, King of the Belgians
1993 'Fourth State Reform' Regions and Communities in Belgium obtain the legal right to enter into treaties; direct elections in Communities and Regions initiated

1993 Nelson Mandela, South African lawyer and anti-apartheid activist, freed after twenty-seven years in prison on Robben Island; receives with De Klerk, Prime Minister of South Africa, the Nobel Prize for Peace

1993-1994 Genocide in Rwanda; extremist Hutu's murder 1 million Tutsi's and moderate Hutu's

1993-1995 'Yugoslav Wars' Civil wars between Bosnians, Croats, Montenegrians, Serbs and Slovenes, with ethnic cleansing on each side; result in new sovereign territories and economic disruption

1993-2001 Bill Clinton, President of the United States of America

1994 'Israel-Jordan Treaty of Peace' makes Jordan the second Arab country to normalise relations with Israel

1994 *Apartheid* ends; Nelson Mandela sworn in as President of the Republic of South Africa

1995 World Trade Organization (WTO) established in Geneva; to remove trade barriers and resolve trade conflicts

1995 EU enlarged with Austria, Finland and Sweden

1995 'Srebrenica Massacre' Killing of eight thousand Bosnian men and boys around Srebrenica (Bosn. & Herz.) by Serbian Army despite the presence of a contingent of Dutch peacekeepers

1995 Armistice in Bosnia and Herzegovina

1996-2002 Taliban succeeds in taking power in Afghanistan

1997 Sovereignty of Hong Kong transferred from UK to China

1999 NATO bombs Yugoslavia to force Serbian Army to leave Kosovo; restoration of Kosovo's autonomy

2000 Henri, Grand Duke of Luxembourg, succeeds his father Jean, who abdicates

2000-2008 Vladimir Putin, President of the Russian Federation

2001 '9/11' Suicide attacks by Al-Qaeda destroy the World Trade Center in New York, killing three thousand people; President George W. Bush embarks on 'The Global War on Terror'

2001-2003 'Fifth State Reform' Powers transferred to Regions regarding agriculture, foreign trade, finance and taxes in Belgium

2001-2008 George W. Bush, President of the United States of America

2002 Euro (€) replaces national currencies in twelve EU member states

2002 Crown Prince William-Alexander marries Argentinian Máxima Zorreguieta, Princess of The Netherlands

2002 Pim Fortuyn, Dutch sociologist and politician, controversial for his views on Islam, murdered; first political murder in The Netherlands since the killing of De Witt brothers in 1672

2003 'Iraq War' Invasion of Iraq by US troops under the leadership of President George W. Bush and UK troops under Prime Minister Tony Blair, in search for weapons of mass destruction; dictator Saddam Hussein of Iraq removed from power

2004 Princess Juliana dies

2004 2004 EU sees its biggest expansion with membership for Cyprus, Malta and eight former Eastern Bloc countries

2004 Dutch film director Theo van Gogh's movie *Submission* criticises the treatment of women under Islamic law

2004 Voting power for non-EU citizens in Belgium

2004 Theo van Gogh murdered

2004 Prince Bernhard dies

Low Countries	Wider World
2005 Surinam becomes member of the Netherlands Language Union, along with Belgium and The Netherlands	
2006 Netherlands' Army participates in NATO mission in Afghanistan	
	2007 Addition of Romania and Bulgaria increases the number of EU members to twenty-seven
2007 A single issue party for animal rights gains seats for the first time in a parliament, in The Netherlands	
	2008 Predominantly Caucasian population of the US elects the African-American Barack Hussein Obama as President of the United States of America
	2008 Lehman Brothers, global financial services firm, declares largest bankruptcy in US history; financial markets react badly, leading to a global economic crisis
2009 'Treaty of Lisbon' amends constitutional basis of EU; moves from unanimity to double majority voting, creates the position of President of the European Council	
2009 Herman van Rompuy, Belgian politician, elected as first President of the European Council	
2010 Netherlands Antilles dissolved; Curaçao becomes a constituent country of the Kingdom of The Netherlands	
2010 Mark Rutte, Dutch politician, first Liberal Prime Minister in The Netherlands for nearly one hundred years	

'The Sea, the Sea splashes on, in endless undulation'
Willem Kloos, Dutch poet

Appendices

National Anthems

The Brabançonne

The Brabançonne is the national anthem of Belgium. The anthem was originally written in French. Now the anthem has also a Dutch and a German version.
The Brabançonne was written by Jeneval, an opera singer of French origin, engaged by the Brussels Opera in 1830, where the revolution started, which led to the independence of Belgium.
The Dutch version was approved in 1938.

O dierbaar België
O heilig land der Vaad'ren
Onze ziel en ons hart zijn u gewijd.
Aanvaard ons kracht en het bloed van onze ad'ren,
Wees ons doel in arbeid en in strijd.
Bloei, o land, in eendracht niet te breken;
Wees immer u zelf en ongeknecht,
Het woord getrouw, dat g' onbevreesd moogt spreken:
Voor Vorst, voor Vrijheid en voor Recht.

The Wilhelmus

The Wilhelmus is the national anthem of The Netherlands and the oldest anthem in the world.
Although it was not recognised as the official national anthem until 1932, it has always been popular with the Dutch and re-surfaced on several occasions in the course of Dutch history before gaining its present status.

Like many anthems, *the Wilhelmus* originated in the national struggle to achieve independence. It tells of William of Orange, his life and why he is fighting against the King of Spain. As a result the anthem is written in the first person perspective, as if it were sung by William himself.

The anthem consists of 15 stanzas, of which the first letters of each stanza form the acrostic *Willem of Nassov*. The text is attributed to Marnix van St Aldegonde, who is supposed to have written the anthem between 1570 and 1572.

Of *the Wilhelmus*, normally the first stanza is sung, sometimes followed by the sixth stanza.

First Stanza

Wilhelmus van Nassouwe ben ik, van Duitsen bloed,
den vaderland getrouwe blijf ik tot in den dood.
Een Prinse van Oranje ben ik, vrij onverveerd,
den Koning van Hispanje heb ik altijd geëerd.

Sixth stanza

Mijn schild ende betrouwen zijt Gij, o God mijn Heer,
op U zo wil ik bouwen, verlaat mij nimmermeer.
Dat ik doch vroom mag blijven, uw dienaar t'aller stond,
de tirannie verdrijven die mij mijn hart doorwondt.

Territories and Trading Posts

Belgium

Free state / Belgian Congo (Congo)	1885-1960
Ruanda-Urundi (Rwanda Burundi)	1924-1962
Santo Tomás (Guatemala)	1843-1854
Tien-Tsin (China)	1902-1931

The Netherlands

Ambon (Indonesia)	1605-1949
Arakan (Burma)	1608-1683
Aruba (Kingdom of The Netherlands)	1665-1986
Banda (Indonesia)	1621-1949
Bantam (Indonesia)	1596-1949
Batavia (Indonesia)	1619-1949
Bengal (Bangladesh)	1607-1757
Berbice (Suriname)	1627-1796
Bonaire (The Netherlands)	1633-1954
Brazil	1630-1654
Cape of Good Hope (South Africa)	1652-1795
Ceylon (Sri Lanka)	1656-1796
Cochin (India)	1539-1819
Coromandel (India)	1605-1784
Curaçao (Kingdom of The Netherlands)	1634-1954
Desjima (Japan)	1640-1854
Essequibo-Demerary (Suriname)	1665-1814
Elmina (Ghana)	1637-1872
Formosa (Taiwan)	1624-1662
Ghana	1638-1871
Malabar (India)	1658-1795
Malay (Malaysia)	1641-1828
Mauritius	1598-1710
Makassar (Indonesia)	1598-1949
New Amsterdam (United States of America)	1625-1674
New Guinea (Indonesia)	1660-1963
Saba (The Netherlands)	1632-1954
San Thomé (Sào Thomé et Principe)	1641-1649
Sao Paolo de Luanda (Angola)	1637-1648
Semarang (Indonesia)	1675-1949
Suriname	1667-1975
Sint Helena (Britain)	1645-1659

Sint Maarten (Kingdom of The Netherlands)	1648-1954
Sint Eustatius (The Netherlands)	1636-1954
Timor (Indonesia)	1650-1949

Present Provinces of the Low Countries

Belgium

Capital region:
Brussels

Flemish region:
Antwerp (Antw.)
East Flanders (E. Flan.)
Flemish Brabant (Fl. Bra.)
Flemish Limburg (Fl. Lim.)
West Flanders (W. Flan.)

Walloon region:
Hainaut (Hain.)
Liège (Lièg.)
Luxembourg (Wal. Lux.)
Namur (Nam.)
Walloon Brabant (Wal. Bra.)

The Netherlands

Groningen (Gro.)
Friesland (Fri.)
Drenthe (Dre.)
Overijssel (Ove.)
Flevoland (Fle.)
Gelderland (Gel.)
North-Holland (N. Hol.)
South-Holland (S. Hol.)
Utrecht (Utr.)
North-Brabant (N. Bra.)
Limburg (N. Lim.)
Zeeland (Zee.)

Bibliography

ALLEN, ROBERT C., *The British Industrial Revolution in Global Perspective* (Cambridge, 2009)

ANDRONICOS, MANOLIS & CAWKWELL, GEORGE & DELL, HARRY J. & EDSON, CHARLES F., *Philip of Macedon* (Athens, 1980)

ANSARY, TAMINN, *Destiny Disrupted, a History of the World through Islamic Eyes* (New York, 2009)

BARLETT, ROBERT, *The making of Europe, Conquest, Colonization and Cultural Change 950-1350* (Princeton, New Jersey, 1993)

BERNSTEIN, WILLIAM J., *A Splendid Exchange, how Trade Shaped the World* (New York, 2008)

CHENG, PEI-KAIi & LESTZ, MICHAELl, *The Search for Modern China, a documentary collection* (New York, 1999)

CHUA, AMY, *Day of Empire, how Hyper Powers rise to Global Dominance – and why they fall* (New York, 2009)

COURTAULD, GEORGE, *Pocket Book of Patriotism, the History of Great Britain and the World* (London, 2004)

FADHI, MOHAMMAD ALI, *Memories of World War II in Libya* (Misurata, Libya, 2005)

FREELY, JOHN, *The Grand Turk, Sultan Mehmet II* (New York, 2009)

FUKUYAMA, FRANCIS, *The Originals of Political Order, from Prehuman Times to the French Revolution* (New York, 2011)

HANSEN, VALERIE, *The Open Empire, a History of China to 1600* (New York, 2000)

HOLLAND, TOM, *Millennium, the End of the World and the Forging of Christendom* (London, 2008)

HOLLAND, TOM, *Persian Fire, the First World Empire and the Battle for the West* (New York, 2007)

HOLLAND, TOM, *Rubicon, the Triumph and Tragedy of the Roman Republic* (London, 2003)

ISRAEL, JONATHAN, *The Dutch Republic, its Rise, Greatness, and Fall 1477-1806* (Oxford, 1995)

JARDIN, LISA, *Going Dutch, how England plundered Holland's Glory*, (New York, 2008)

KAPLAN, ROBERT D., *Monsoon, the Indian Ocean and the Future of American Power (New York, 2010)*

KISSINGER, HENRY, *On China* (New York, 2011)

KULKE, HERMAN & ROTHERMUND, DIETMAR, *A History of India* (New Dehli, 1986)

MAHBUBANI, KISHORE, *The New Asia Hemisphere, the Irresistible Shift of Global Power to the East* (New York, 2008)
McKITTERICK, ROSAMOND, *Charlemagne, the Formation of a European Identity* (Cambridge, 2008)
NORWICH, JOHN JULIUS, *The Middle Sea, a History of the Mediterranean* (New York, 2006)
PINCUS, STEVE, *1688 The First Modern Revolution* (London, 2009)
SCHAMA, SIMON, *The Embarrassment of Riches, an Interpretation of Dutch Culture in the Golden Age* (London, 1987)
SCHOPPA, R. KEITH, *The Columbia Guide to Modern Chinese History* (New York, 1943)
TEMPLE, ROBERT K. G., *The Genius of China, 3000 Years of Science, Discovery & Invention* (London, 1986)
WILSON, PETER H., *The Thirty Years War, Europe's Tragedy* (Cambridge, 2009)
ZAMOYSKI, ADAM, *Rites of Peace, the Fall of Napoleon and the Congress of Vienna* (New York, 2007

Indexes

Art & Science

Constructions

Discoveries

Inventions

Military Conflicts

Peoples

Persons

Philosophy & Religion

Treaties

De volgekleurde gedeelten hebben deel uitgemaakt van den Duitschen Bond; n.l. Limburg als hertogdom van 1839-1866, Luxemburg in zijn geheel tot 1839, het Oostelijk gedeelte tot 1866.
Kerkelijke Indeeling van 1853 (Ned.)
Zetel van den Aartsbisschop
Zetel van een Bisschop.
Grens bij den eersten vrede van Parijs.
Taalgrenzen in België.
Schaal 1: 2.200.000
SCHIERMONNIKOOG
ROTTUM
AMELAND
TERSCHELLING
VLIELAND
TESSEL
Emden
Delfzijl
GRONINGEN
Groningen
Leeuwarden
Harlingen
FRIESLAND
Tinaarloo
Assen
Sneek
Borger
DRENTE
Helder
WIERINGEN
Stavoren
Koevorden
NOORD-
Enkhuizen
Alkmaar
URK
SCHOKLD.
HOLLAND
Zwolle
OVERIJSEL
Ymuiden
MARKEN
Haarlem
Amsterdam
1839
Kamp
Almeloo
Loo
Deventer
Enschede
Leiden
Zutfen
Kp
Utrecht
Scheveningen
ZUID-
GELDERLAND
Den Haag
UTRECHT
Delft
Gouda
Arnhem
Hoek
Rotterdam
Wageningen
Tiel
Hellevoetsluis
Dordrecht
Gorkum
Nijmegen
HOLLAND
Kleef
den Bosch
Wezel
NOORD.-BRABANT
Breda
Tilbg
Middelbg.
ZEELAND
Vlissingen
Baarle Hertog
Eindhoven
3
4
5
6
7
54
53
52